D0036685

Presented to:

Betty

By:

Gail

Date:

March 6, 2010

A Pocketful of
PROMISES
for Women

Betty,

May these promises come to fruition in these uncertain times!

Love
Gail

HONOR ⓗⒷ BOOKS

FROM DAVID C. COOK

A POCKETFUL OF PROMISES FOR WOMEN
Published by Honor Books®, an imprint of
David C. Cook
4050 Lee Vance View
Colorado Springs, CO 80918 U.S.A.

David C. Cook Distribution Canada
55 Woodslee Avenue, Paris, Ontario, Canada N3L 3E5

David C. Cook U.K., Kingsway Communications
Eastbourne, East Sussex BN23 6NT, England

David C. Cook and the graphic circle C logo
are registered trademarks of Cook Communications Ministries.

All rights reserved. Except for brief excerpts for review purposes,
no part of this book may be reproduced or used in any form
without written permission from the publisher.

Unless otherwise noted, Scripture quotations are taken from the King James Version of
the Bible. Scripture quotations marked NASB are taken from the NEW AMERICAN
STANDARD BIBLE®, Copyright © 1960, 1962, 1963, 1968, 1971, 1972, 1973, 1975,
1977, 1995 by The Lockman Foundation. Used by permission; ASV are taken from the
American Standard Version © Copyright 1901. Public Domain; CEV are taken from the
Contemporary English Version © 1995 by American Bible Society. Used by permission;
NIV is taken from the HOLY BIBLE, NEW INTERNATIONAL VERSION®. Copyright
© 1973, 1978, 1984 International Bible Society. Used by permission of Zondervan. All
rights reserved; TLB are taken from The Living Bible, © 1971, Tyndale House Publishers,
Wheaton, IL 60189. Used by permission; AMP are taken from the Amplified® Bible,
Copyright © 1954, 1958, 1962, 1964, 1965, 1987 by The Lockman Foundation. Used
by permission; NKJV are taken from the New King James Version®. Copyright © 1982 by
Thomas Nelson, Inc. Used by permission. All rights reserved; RSV are taken from the
Revised Standard Version of the Bible, copyrighted © 1946, 1952, and 1971 by the
Division of Christian Education of the Churches of Christ in the United States of
America, and are used by permission. All rights reserved; NRSV are taken from the New
Revised Standard Version of the Bible, copyrighted by the Division of Christian
Education of the National Council of the Churches of Christ in the United States of
America, and are used by permission; NLT are taken from the New Living Translation
copyright © 1996 by Tyndale Charitable Trust. Used by permission of Tyndale House
Publishers; marked NCV are taken from the New Century Version®. NCV™ Copyright
© 1987, 1988, 1991 by Thomas Nelson, Inc. Used by permission. All rights reserved.

ISBN 978-1-56292-162-0

© 2004 by Bordon Books

Developed by Bordon Books
6532 E. 71 Street, Suite 105
Tulsa, OK 74133

Printed in the United States of America

First Edition 2004

10 11 12 13 14 15 16 17

042608

Contents

Introduction

Perhaps you've experienced the joy of friendship with someone who knows you, understands you, and loves you when you're not at your best. Most likely, you found they offered unconditional love and understanding no matter what circumstance or situation you found yourself in. Imagine your excitement in sharing your life and joy with them. God wants to be that friend to you. You don't have to pick up the telephone or drive across town to be with Him. He is as close as the mention of His name.

God is that encouraging friend, comforter, and the One who can understand you, even when you can't. He wants to be your personal God and confidant. He has given you promises for your life, and He keeps His promises forever. Discover God's voice through His letters to you in *A Pocketful of Promises for Women*.

When we take hold of God's promises, we have all we need to find health and happiness, confidence and contentment, both for this life and the life to come. *A Pocketful of Promises for Women* includes a letter from God to you from daily living that you can apply to your own life. You will also find scriptures and encouraging quotes to help you trust God with even the most important areas of your life. Allow Him to fill you with hope, courage, understanding, and strength through this book. •

How to Use *A Pocketful of Promises* in Your Quiet Time

A Pocketful of Promises is more than a book of scriptures arranged by topic. Within these pages you will find an encouraging letter from God about each topic, scriptures that offer hope and inspire you to face life's challenges, and quotes to motivate you to rise above the conflict in your heart and mind.

You can use this book in a variety of ways. The following are some suggestions to help you begin to use *A Pocketful of Promises* in your quiet time.

1. Within the table of contents, which we have conveniently placed at the front of the book, locate the topic you are facing today.

2. Read the section from the topic you are interested in. Break the verse into sections, then ponder and mull over what they mean and are saying to you about God, His character, your life, and your faith.

3. Choose one specific verse to meditate on.

4. Put that verse in your memory, and think about it throughout the day.

5. Personalize the scripture by adding personal pronouns—me, my, I, etc.—in place of you, we, and they. Remember, you are in a personal relationship with the God who loves you, so expect Him to speak directly and personally to you.

6. Consider writing down in a notebook what God has shown you about each promise. How does it change your thoughts, feelings, and motivation concerning your situation or circumstances?

Discover what God has to say to you about your life. He cares for you and wants you to know it. Allow Him to fill you with hope, courage, understanding, and strength through this book. Have a daily quiet time where you and God can spend regular quality time together. You will find it a practice that will greatly benefit your life.

GOD'S
PROMISES
FOR MY . . .

wonderful sister
Betty

DOUBTS

My Daughter,

I know you are struggling with doubt, but deep inside your spirit I have given you faith to move mountains. Let My precious promises wash your doubts away. I will never leave you, fail you, or forsake you. I am always with you; you are never alone. When you feel like giving up, cast your care and burdens upon Me. Rest in My arms and trust Me to take care of all that concerns you. I love you. Lift your eyes to the Heavens, for I am your help. Call on Me and I will restore you. Hope in Me, for I am here.

~Your Father

God has said, "I will never, *never*
fail you nor forsake you."
HEBREWS 13:5 TLB

Jesus answered . . . "Truly I say to you, whoever
says to this mountain, 'Be taken up and
cast into the sea,' and does not doubt in
his heart, but believes that what he says
is going to happen, it will be granted him."
MARK 11:22–23 NASB

"Yes, be bold and strong! Banish fear
and doubt! For remember, the Lord
your God is with you wherever you go."
JOSHUA 1:9 TLB

Let us hold firmly to the hope that
we have confessed, because we can
trust God to do what he promised.
HEBREWS 10:23 NCV

Jesus answered and said to them, "Truly I say
to you, if you have faith and do not doubt, you
will not only do what was done to the fig tree,
but even if you say to this mountain, 'Be taken
up and cast into the sea,' it will happen."
MATTHEW 21:21 NASB

"When the Son of Man returns, you will know
it beyond all doubt. It will be as evident as
the lightning that flashes across the sky."
LUKE 17:24 NLT

I *am with you always,*
even to the end of the age.

DREAMS

Dear Child,

Dream big dreams. Many of your dreams are My dreams for your life. I share your excitement for the future, and I have big plans for you. I have held them in My heart since before you were born. I want to see them become a reality as much as you do. Trust Me to fulfill My plans for your life. I have a path in mind for you to follow. Trust and follow Me on your journey. With Me, all things are possible...only believe!

~God

"I know the plans that I have for you," declares
the LORD, "plans for welfare and not for
calamity to give you a future and a hope."

PhpJEREMIAH 29:11 NASB

He who began a good work in you will carry it
on to completion until the day of Christ Jesus.

PHILIPPIANS 1:6 NIV

When dreams come true at last,
there is life and joy.

PROVERBS 13:12 TLB

Delight yourself in the LORD;
and He will give you the desires of your heart.

PSALM 37:4 NASB

"In the last days it will be, God declares,
that I will pour out my Spirit upon all flesh,
and your sons and your daughters shall
prophesy, and your young men shall see visions,
and your old men shall dream dreams."

ACTS 2:17 NRSV

Depend on the Lord in whatever you do,
and your plans will succeed.

PROVERBS 16:3 NCV

*Don't ask yourself what the world needs;
ask yourself what makes you come alive.
And then go and do that.
Because what the world needs are
people who have come alive.*

 # FAMILY

My Precious Child,

I am your Father—you belong to Me. I love you with an everlasting love. You are created in My image, and you favor Me. I have filled you with My wisdom and direction. Even as you wouldn't let someone you love fall, I won't let you fall. I want you to come close to Me. Talk to Me and tell Me your heart, as I am listening. With patience I wait for you to include Me. You are family, a part of My heart.

~Your Heavenly
Father

We who have been made holy by Jesus, now
have the same Father he has. That is why
Jesus is not ashamed to call us his brothers.

HEBREWS 2:11 TLB

"I will not leave you as orphans;
I will come to you."

JOHN 14:18 NASB

See how very much our heavenly Father
loves us, for he allows us to be called
his children, and we really are!

1 JOHN 3:1 NLT

Then, even if I am delayed, you will
know how to live in the family of God.
That family is the church of the living God,
the support and foundation of the truth.

1 TIMOTHY 3:15 NCV

"I will be your father, and you will be my sons
and daughters, says the Lord Almighty."

2 CORINTHIANS 6:18 NCV

For this reason I bow my knees to the Father
of our Lord Jesus Christ, from whom the
whole family in heaven and earth is named.

EPHESIANS 3:14–15 NKJV

Family is God's idea.

FINANCES

My Daughter,

I am the supplier of your needs.
Although I know what you need before
you ask, I still like to have you come to
Me and ask, for I am your provider.
Just as an earthly father desires to give
good gifts to his children, so I desire to
give good gifts to you. I will open the
windows of heaven and pour out a
blessing for you. I have made a
provision for your life, and I desire to
see you become a blessing to others, also.

~Your Provider

"Therefore I say to you, do not worry about
your life . . . Look at the birds of the air,
for they neither sow nor reap nor gather
into barns; yet your heavenly Father feeds them.
Are you not of more value than they?"
MATTHEW 6:25-26 NKJV

It is he who will supply all your needs
from his riches in glory, because of
what Christ Jesus has done for us.
PHILIPPIANS 4:19 TLB

He who gathers by labor will increase.
PROVERBS 13:11 NKJV

"Bring all the tithes into the storehouse so there
will be enough food in my Temple. If you do,"
says the LORD Almighty, "I will open the windows
of heaven for you. I will pour out a blessing
so great you won't have enough room to
take it in! Try it! Let me prove it to you!"
MALACHI 3:10 NLT

God is able to make all grace abound toward you,
that you, always having all sufficiency in all *things*,
may have an abundance for every good work.
2 CORINTHIANS 9:8 NKJV

He will give you all you need from day
to day if you live for him and make the
Kingdom of God your primary concern.
MATTHEW 6:33 NLT

*He who is plenteously provided for from
within needs but little from without.*

19

FUTURE

My Daughter,

I have wonderfully planned your future, and I have filled your life with potential and purpose. My prayer is that you would look to your future with as much pleasure and expectation as I do. My plans are for you to succeed and bring into existence all you were destined for. Hope with earnest expectation for all I have for you. Your future is in My hands, and it can happen as I have dreamed. I love you.

~Almighty God

It's in Christ that we find out who we are and
what we are living for. Long before we first heard
of Christ and got our hopes up, he had his eye
on us, had designs on us for glorious living,

EPHESIANS 1:11 THE MESSAGE

I know the plans I have for you, says the Lord.
They are plans for good and not for evil,
to give you a future and a hope.

JEREMIAH 29:11 TLB

"At the time I have decided, my words will come true.
You can trust what I say about the future. It may take
a long time, but keep on waiting—it will happen!"

HABAKKUK 2:3 CEV

Mark the blameless man, and observe the upright;
for the future of that man is peace.

PSALM 37:37 NKJV

Surely goodness and lovingkindness
will follow me all the days of my life,
and I will dwell in the house of the LORD forever.

PSALM 23:6 NASB

The Lord will certainly deliver and draw me to
Himself from every assault of evil. He will preserve
and bring me safe unto His heavenly kingdom.

2 TIMOTHY 4:18 AMP

*F*uture contingents cannot be certain to us, because
we know them as such. They can be certain only to
God whose understanding is in eternity above time.
Just as a man going along a road does not see those
who come after him; but the man who sees the whole
road from a height sees all those who are going
along the road at the same time.

LIFE

My Beloved,

I have given you the choice of life or death. However, I desire for you to choose My ways—eternal life through Christ Jesus. When you choose Me and follow My commandments, you will find yourself eternally nestled in My hand. As long as you choose to follow Me, I will fill you with my joy and give you a long life. Your life is a joy to Me, and you bring Me great pleasure when you stay close to Me. You will receive favor when you seek Me and stay on the path I've set before you. Choose Me.

~Your Life-giver

"Choose to love the LORD your God and to obey him
and commit yourself to him, for he is your life.
Then you will live long in the land the LORD swore
to give your ancestors Abraham, Isaac, and Jacob."

DEUTERONOMY 30:20 NLT

You will teach me how to live a holy life.
Being with you will fill me with joy; at your
right hand I will find pleasure forever.

PSALM 16:11 NCV

My child, listen and accept what I say.
Then you will have a long life.

PROVERBS 4:10 NCV

I give eternal life to them, and
they will never perish; and no one
will snatch them out of My hand.

JOHN 10:28 NASB

If the Spirit of Him Who raised up Jesus from
the dead dwells in you, [then] He Who raised
up Christ Jesus from the dead will also restore
to life your mortal (short-lived, perishable)
bodies through His Spirit Who dwells in you.

ROMANS 8:11 AMP

Whoever finds me finds life and
receives favor from the LORD.

PROVERBS 8:35 NIV

Life is God's novel. Let Him write it.

MARRIAGE

My Daughter,

If you and your spouse will build your marriage on the foundation of My love, it will grow stronger each day. Remain patient and kind toward each other, giving to each other. Live your marriage with honor and esteem it as precious and worthy of great price. As you allow love to rule in your marriage, you please Me. When you agree, your prayers go unhindered. Ask of Me that I may give you a marriage that honors Me.

~Your Covenant
Keeper

Let marriage be held in honor
(esteemed worthy, precious, of great price,
and especially dear) in all things.
HEBREWS 13:4 AMP

Have unity of spirit, sympathy, love for one another,
a tender heart, and a humble mind. Do not
repay evil for evil or abuse for abuse; but, on the
contrary, repay with a blessing. It is for this that
you were called—that you might inherit a blessing.
1 PETER 3:8-9 NRSV

Love has been perfected among us in this: that
we may have boldness in the day of judgment;
because as He is, so are we in this world. There is
no fear in love; but perfect love casts out fear.
1 JOHN 4:17-18 NKJV

He *who* finds a wife finds a good *thing*,
and obtains favor from the LORD.
PROVERBS 18:22 NKJV

As the Scriptures say, "A man leaves his
father and mother to get married, and he
becomes like one person with his wife."
EPHESIANS 5:31 CEV

Husbands, in the same way be considerate
as you live with your wives, and treat them
with respect as the weaker partner and as
heirs with you of the gracious gift of life,
so that nothing will hinder your prayers.
1 PETER 3:7 NIV

❧

*A successful marriage is an edifice
that must be rebuilt every day.*

MISTAKES

My Daughter,

If you stumble and fall, I will help you up. Humble yourself before Me—for I am rich in mercy toward you. When you make a mistake and fall into sin, be quick to tell Me about it so I can forgive you and we can go forward as though it never existed. I don't remember your failures, only your successes.

~Your Forgiving
　　Father

"If my people, who are called by my name,
are sorry for what they have done, if they
pray and obey me and stop their evil ways,
I will hear them from heaven. I will forgive
their sin, and I will heal their land."

2 CHRONICLES 7:14 NCV

Depart from evil, and do good;
and dwell for evermore.

PSALM 37:27 ASV

If we confess our sins, he is faithful and
just and will forgive us our sins and
purify us from all unrighteousness.

1 JOHN 1:9 NIV

My little children, I am telling you this so that
you will stay away from sin. But if you sin, there
is someone to plead for you before the Father.
His name is Jesus Christ, the one who is all
that is good and who pleases God completely.

1 JOHN 2:1 TLB

People cannot see their own mistakes.
Forgive me for my secret sins.

PSALM 19:12 NCV

"Those who err in mind will know the truth."

ISAIAH 29:24 NASB

*The greatest mistake we make is living in
constant fear that we will make one.*

PAST

Dear One,

Look forward instead of backward. Your future is ahead of you and the past is behind you. I am the creator of new things. When you came to Me, former things passed away and all things were created new. You are growing and becoming new through your relationship with Me. Let go of the past and press forward to your new adventure in faith.

~Your Hope

"Forget the former things; do not dwell on the past.
See, I am doing a new thing! Now it springs up;
do you not perceive it? I am making a way
in the desert and streams in the wasteland."

ISAIAH 43:18-19 NIV

"Behold, I create new heavens and
a new earth; and the former things shall
not be remembered or come into mind."

ISAIAH 65:17 RSV

Surely it was for my welfare that I had
great bitterness; but you have held back
my life from the pit of destruction, for you
have cast all my sins behind your back.

ISAIAH 38:17 NRSV

God will wipe away every tear from their eyes;
there shall be no more death, nor sorrow,
nor crying. There shall be no more pain,
for the former things have passed away.

REVELATION 21:4 NKJV

Dear brothers, I am still not all I should be
but I am bringing all my energies to bear
on this one thing: Forgetting the past
and looking forward to what lies ahead.

PHILIPPIANS 3:13 TLB

Those who become Christians become new persons.
They are not the same anymore, for the
old life is gone. A new life has begun!

2 CORINTHIANS 5:17 NLT

*I see not a step before me as I tread on
another year; but I've left the Past in God's
keeping—The Future, His mercy shall clear.
What looks dark in the distance may brighten
as I draw near.*

PROVISION

My Daughter,

I have promised to withhold no good thing from you, for you have favor and grace in My sight. I see the big picture of your life and will take good care of you always. Through the twists and turns of life, I will be with you and give you My provision. Remember that I can make a way when there seems to be no way. Look up and hold your head high because you are My child, and I shall supply all your needs.

~Father God

The LORD is my shepherd, I shall not want.

PSALM 23:1 RSV

Your Father knoweth what things
ye have need of, before ye ask him.

MATTHEW 6:8 KJV

His divine power hath given unto us all things
that pertain unto life and godliness.

2 PETER 1:3 KJV

My God shall supply all your need according
to his riches in glory by Christ Jesus.

PHILIPPIANS 4:19 KJV

Those who look to the LORD will
have every good thing.

PSALM 34:10 NCV

The LORD will give grace and glory: no good thing
will he withhold from them that walk uprightly.

PSALM 84:11 KJV

*The Lord my pasture shall prepare,
And feed me with a shepherd's care;
His presence shall my wants supply,
And guard me with a watchful eye.*

REST

My Daughter,

Let me teach you the next step of faith for My yoke is easy and My burden is light. My gentleness can make you great. My humility can bring peace to your soul, and My Spirit can fill you with life-giving strength. For it is in Me that you will receive the wisdom to know how much to do and the strength to do it. If you will come near to Me, like a shepherd, I will lead you to the green pastures and still waters of My presence.

~Your Peace

You let me rest in fields of green grass.
You lead me to streams of peaceful water,
and you refresh my life. You are true to your
name, and you lead me along the right paths.

PSALM 23:2-3 CEV

"Come to me, all who labor and are
heavy laden, and I will give you rest."

MATTHEW 11:28 RSV

He said, My presence shall go *with thee*,
and I will give thee rest.

EXODUS 33:14 ASV

There remains, then, a Sabbath-rest
for the people of God.

HEBREWS 4:9 NIV

"Accept my teachings and learn from me,
because I am gentle and humble in spirit,
and you will find rest for your lives."

MATTHEW 11:29 NCV

My people will live in a peaceful habitation,
and in secure dwellings and in
undisturbed resting places.

ISAIAH 32:18 NASB

For he is a mixture of gravity and waggery.
For he knows that God is his Saviour.
For there is nothing sweeter than his peace
when at rest.

GOD'S PROMISES WHEN I EXPERIENCE . . .

CONFLICT

Child of Mine,

You may face many problems in your lifetime, but know that I am able to deliver you from all of them. When you pray, forgive those you hold anything against so you can experience the fullness of My forgiveness toward you and enjoy the freedom that comes from letting go of past offenses. When you demonstrate kindness, you will rise far above your enemies, possibly even making them friends. Place your cares in My hands. I'll give you the strength to embrace conflict with kindness.

~Your Resolution

Even when we were God's enemies, he made peace
with us, because his Son died for us. Yet something
even greater than friendship is ours. Now that we are
at peace with God, we will be saved by his Son's life.

ROMANS 5:10 CEV

Cast out the scorner, and contention shall go out;
yea, strife and reproach shall cease.

PROVERBS 22:10 KJV

You hide them in the shelter of your presence, safe
from those who conspire against them. You shelter
them in your presence, far from accusing tongues.

PSALM 31:20 NLT

Our struggle is not against enemies of blood and flesh,
but against the rulers, against the authorities, against
the cosmic powers of this present darkness, against
the spiritual forces of evil in the heavenly places.

EPHESIANS 6:12 NRSV

This is what you were called to do, because Christ
suffered for you and gave you an example to
follow. So you should do as he did. . . . People
insulted Christ, but he did not insult them in return.
Christ suffered, but he did not threaten. He let God,
the One who judges rightly, take care of him.

1 PETER 2:21, 23 NCV

When God approves of your life, even your
enemies will end up shaking your hand.

PROVERBS 16:7 THE MESSAGE

◉

*The harder the conflict,
the more glorious the triumph.*

DEPRESSION

Dear Child,

I will never give up on you. My joy is your strength when a cloud of depression tries to discourage your soul. Your life has meaning and purpose, which I have created in you. When you trust in Me, I will give you strength to go forward. The rain of darkness will subside, and sunshine will fill your soul. Count on Me.

~Your Joy

The ropes of death surrounded me; the floods of destruction swept over me. The grave wrapped its ropes around me; death itself stared me in the face. But in my distress I cried out to the LORD; yes, I prayed to my God for help. He heard me from his sanctuary; my cry reached his ears. . . . He reached down from heaven and rescued me; he drew me out of deep waters.

PSALM 18:4-6, 16 NLT

"In my great trouble I cried to the Lord and he answered me; from the depths of death I called, and Lord, you heard me!"

JONAH 2:2 TLB

The LORD also will be a refuge for the oppressed, a refuge in times of trouble.

PSALM 9:9 NKJV

Cast your burden upon the LORD and He will sustain you; He will never allow the righteous to be shaken.

PSALM 55:22 NASB

"With the loving mercy of our God, a new day from heaven will dawn upon us. It will shine on those who live in darkness, in the shadow of death. It will guide us into the path of peace."

LUKE 1:78-79 NCV

Who executes justice for the oppressed, Who gives food to the hungry. The Lord sets free the prisoners, the Lord opens the eyes of the blind, the Lord lifts up those who are bowed down, the Lord loves the [uncompromisingly] righteous (those upright in heart and in right standing with Him).

PSALM 146:7-8 AMP

❧

Abide with me—fast falls the eventide;
The darkness deepens: Lord, with me abide;
When other helpers fail, and comforts flee,
Help of the helpless, O abide with me.

39

# FAILURE

My Daughter,

Take your focus off failure. I am your shield and your glory. Hold your head high, and remember who you are in Christ. Because of what My Son did for you, I see you as holy, righteous, perfect. If you'll just trust in Me and accept My help, there is nothing you can't accomplish. I am the Lord your God, your redemption, your help, and your strength.

~God

If the LORD delights in a man's way, he makes his
steps firm; though he stumble, he will not fall,
for the LORD upholds him with his hand.
PSALM 37:23-24 NIV

Do not rejoice over me, O my enemy;
when I fall, I shall rise; when I sit in
darkness, the LORD will be a light to me.
MICAH 7:8 NRSV

Even though good people may be bothered by
trouble seven times, they are never defeated.
PROVERBS 24:16 NCV

LORD, how they have increased who trouble me! Many
are they who rise up against me. Many are they who
say of me, "There is no help for him in God." Selah.
But You, O Lord, are a shield for me, my glory and the
One who lifts up my head. I cried to the LORD with
my voice, and He heard me from His holy hill. Selah
PSALM 3:1-4 NKJV

When you pass through the waters, I will be with
you; and when you pass through the rivers, they
will not sweep over you. When you walk through
the fire, you will not be burned; the flames
will not set you ablaze. For I am the LORD,
your God, the Holy One of Israel, your Savior.
ISAIAH 43:2-3 NIV

Bless the LORD, O my soul, and all that is
within me, bless His holy name. . . . Who redeems
your life from the pit, who crowns you with
lovingkindness and compassion; who satisfies your
years with good things, so that your youth is
renewed like the eagle.
PSALM 103:1,4-5 NASB

*Beware succumbing to failure as inevitable; make
it a stepping-stone to success.*

LOSS

Precious Child,

During this difficult time of loss, do not think you are alone. I am with you in your sadness. I want to carry you in your sorrow. You don't have to put on a brave face. Please come to Me in your pain because I long to hold you and comfort you. I am as close to you as your breath. I love you dearly.

~Your Heavenly Father

Praise be to the God and Father of our Lord Jesus Christ, the Father of compassion and the God of all comfort, who comforts us in all our troubles, so that we can comfort those in any trouble with the comfort we ourselves have received from God.

2 CORINTHIANS 1:3-4 NIV

I will comfort them and turn their sorrow into happiness.

JEREMIAH 31:13 CEV

I love the LORD, because He has heard my voice and my supplications. Because He has inclined His ear to me, therefore I will call upon Him as long as I live.

PSALM 116:1-2 NKJV

"Blessed are those who mourn, for they shall be comforted."

MATTHEW 5:4 NASB

He will wipe away all tears from their eyes, and there shall be no more death, nor sorrow, nor crying, nor pain. All of that has gone forever.

REVELATION 21:4 TLB

Regarding the question, friends, that has come up about what happens to those already dead and buried, we don't want you in the dark any longer. First off, you must not carry on over them like people who have nothing to look forward to, as if the grave were the last word. Since Jesus died and broke loose from the grave, God will most certainly bring back to life those who died in Jesus.

1 THESSALONIANS 4:13-14 THE MESSAGE

When Christ brings His cross, He brings his presence; and where He is, none is desolate, and there is no room for despair. As He knows His own, so He knows how to comfort them, using sometimes the very grief itself, and straining it to a sweetness of peace unattainable by those ignorant of sorrow.

43

SELF-PITY

My Love,

It grieves My heart that My children must sometimes suffer, but take courage in knowing that I can work even this situation out for good. When you are tempted to feel sorry for yourself, try to think about all of the blessings I've poured into your life. They may be difficult for you to recognize right now, but start with simply the gift of life, the very breath you breathe, the intricate design of your body. Think about the people I've brought into your life, and be assured that I care so deeply about you that a hair can't fall from your head without My knowing. My love for You will never end, and neither will My blessings. I have great things planned for you—you'll see.

Almighty God

We know that all things work together for good to them that love God, to them who are the called according to his purpose.

ROMANS 8:28 KJV

Godliness with contentment is great gain.

1 TIMOTHY 6:6 NIV

We have troubles all around us, but we are not defeated. We do not know what to do, but we do not give up the hope of living. We are persecuted, but God does not leave us. We are hurt sometimes, but we are not destroyed.

2 CORINTHIANS 4:8-9 NCV

We are His workmanship, created in Christ Jesus for good works.

EPHESIANS 2:10 NASB

I am not telling you this because I need anything. I have learned to be satisfied with the things I have and with everything that happens.

PHILIPPIANS 4:11 NCV

A righteous man may have many troubles, but the LORD delivers him from them all.

PSALM 34:19 NIV

Count your blessings instead of your hurts.

SUFFERING

My Daughter,

Suffering is not pleasant, but I am with you even in the worst circumstances, loving you, holding you up, and giving you strength to get through this difficult time. Rest in My love for you. When you need someone to talk to, come to Me. Let Me embrace you with My peace. Remember, too, that all your brothers and sisters in Christ are also encountering various trials. You are not alone. Don't be afraid to share the heaviness in your heart with them. I designed you to rely upon each other. Be open to accepting My love and comfort in whatever form it may come, and know that I'll never leave you to suffer alone.

~God

Since he himself has now been through
suffering and temptation, he knows what it
is like when we suffer and are tempted,
and he is wonderfully able to help us.
HEBREWS 2:18 TLB

Those who suffer according to God's
will should commit themselves to their
faithful Creator and continue to do good.
1 PETER 4:19 NIV

I will ask the Father, and he will give you another
Counselor, who will never leave you. . . .
No, I will not abandon you as orphans—
I will come to you."
JOHN 14:16, 18 NLT

If I should say, " My foot has slipped,"
Your lovingkindness, O LORD, will hold me up.
When my anxious thoughts multiply within me,
Your consolations delight my soul.
PSALM 94:18–19 NASB

Grace to you and peace from God our Father and
the Lord Jesus Christ. I give thanks to my God
always for you because of the grace of God
that has been given you in Christ Jesus.
1 CORINTHIANS 1:3–4 NRSV

God is our protection and our strength.
He always helps in times of trouble.
PSALM 46:1 NCV

*J*esus did not come to explain away suffering or
remove it. He came to fill it with His presence.

TRAGEDY

My Beloved,

I know the deepest emotions you feel at this time. I desire for you to bring them all to Me—sadness, anger, frustration, or fear. I can handle it. I will not reject you. You may be feeling alone, as if no one could possibly understand what you're going through; but I know everything you're facing, and I understand. I will comfort you and give you strength and wisdom to make it through this time.

~Your Restoration

"The Spirit of the Lord GOD is upon Me, because the
LORD has anointed Me to preach good tidings to the
poor; He has sent Me to heal the brokenhearted,
to proclaim liberty to the captives, and the opening
of the prison to those who are bound; to proclaim
the acceptable year of the LORD, and the day of
vengeance of our God; to comfort all who mourn,
to console those who mourn in Zion, to give them
beauty for ashes, the oil of joy for mourning, the
garment of praise for the spirit of heaviness; that
they may be called trees of righteousness, the
planting of the LORD, that He may be glorified."

ISAIAH 61:1-3 NKJV

Crying may last for a night, but
joy comes in the morning.

PSALM 30:5 NCV

He took our suffering on him and felt
our pain for us. We saw his suffering
and thought God was punishing him.

ISAIAH 53:4 NCV

He heals the brokenhearted and binds up their wounds.

PSALM 147:3 NASB

"Where, O death, is your victory? Where, O death,
is your sting?" The sting of death is sin, and the
power of sin is the law. But thanks be to God, who
gives us the victory through our Lord Jesus Christ.

1 CORINTHIANS 15:55-57 NRSV

"I have told you all this so that you may have
peace in me. Here on earth you will have
many trials and sorrows. But take heart,
because I have overcome the world."

JOHN 16:33 NLT

☙

*There is only one being who can satisfy the
last aching abyss of the human heart, and
that is the Lord Jesus Christ.*

49

GOD'S PROMISES
WHEN
I NEED . . .

ASSURANCE

My Love,

You may feel powerless, small, and lost in the big picture of your life, but I am your place of safety. I have overcome the world, and My overcoming spirit is in you. Depend on Me and I will fill your heart with assurance and peace. Just as a small child puts his hand into the hand of his father to cross the street, put your hand in Mine and I will lead you to a safe haven. I loved you enough to die for you; therefore, you can be victorious in this life and forever. Call on Me and I will answer. I am closer than your very breath.

~Jesus

"I am the LORD, your God, who takes hold of your right hand and says to you, Do not fear; I will help you."
ISAIAH 41:13 NIV

Give your worries to the LORD, and he will take care of you. He will never let good people down.
PSALM 55:22 NCV

Overwhelming victory is ours through Christ who loved us enough to die for us.
ROMANS 8:37 TLB

As far as the east is from the west, so far has He removed our transgressions from us.
PSALM 103:12 NKJV

"Truly, truly, I say to you, he who hears My word, and believes Him who sent Me, has eternal life, and does not come into judgment, but has passed out of death into life."
JOHN 5:24 NASB

Let us draw near to God with a sincere heart in full assurance of faith.
HEBREWS 10:22 NIV

The man who meets every obligation to the family, to society, to the state, to his country, and his God, to the very best measure of his strength and ability, cannot fail of that assurance and quietness that comes of a good conscience, and will seldom fail of the approval of his fellow-men, and will never fail of the reward which is promised to his faithfulness.

COMFORT

My Daughter,

Do not be troubled, but trust in Me. I will open My everlasting arms and hold you up in the midst of the sea of life. Allow My presence to calm your fears. As a mother comforts her child, so I will comfort you. I will not send you away from Me but will draw you close to My heart. Bask in the fullness of how much I love you. No matter what you face in life, remember that I am standing beside you, lifting you up and comforting you with My peace. My grace is sufficient.

~God

The LORD is good, a refuge in times of trouble.
He cares for those who trust in him.

NAHUM 1:7 NIV

Though I am surrounded by troubles, you will bring
me safely through them. You will clench your fist
against my angry enemies! Your power will save me.

PSALM 138:7 TLB

Even when walking through the dark valley of
death I will not be afraid, for you are close
beside me, guarding, guiding all the way.

PSALM 23:4 TLB

"Blessed are those who mourn,
for they will be comforted."

MATTHEW 5:4 NIV

I will not leave you comfortless: I will come to you.

JOHN 14:18 KJV

Praise be to the God and Father of our Lord Jesus
Christ, the Father of compassion and the God of all
comfort, who comforts us in all our troubles, so
that we can comfort those in any trouble with the
comfort we ourselves have received from God.

2 CORINTHIANS 1:3-4 NIV

*God does not comfort us to make us
comfortable, but to make us comforters.*

COMPASSION

My Child,

Cheer up your soul for I do not want you to be disgraced, nor do I want your enemies to rejoice in your defeats. I know the path you should take and am ready to point you in the right direction, no matter how many times you stumble or go astray. Allow My truth to lead you. Remember My unfailing love and compassion, which I have shown you before. I don't see you through your failures; I see you through the eyes of mercy and love. My heart is full of compassion towards you. Please receive and accept My love.

~Your Father

"The LORD your God is gracious and compassionate, and will not turn *His* face away from you if you return to Him."

2 CHRONICLES 30:9 NASB

Through the Lord's mercies we are not consumed, because His compassions fail not.

LAMENTATIONS 3:22 NKJV

Once again you will have compassion on us. You will trample our sins under your feet and throw them into the depths of the ocean!

MICAH 7:19 NLT

He has made His wonderful works to be remembered; the Lord is gracious, merciful, and full of loving compassion.

PSALM 111:4 AMP

The LORD is good to everyone. He showers compassion on all his creation.

PSALM 145:9 NLT

The Lord is full of compassion and mercy.

JAMES 5:11 NIV

Teach me to feel another's woe,
To hide the fault I see;
That mercy I to others show,
That mercy show to me.

CONFIDENCE

My Daughter,

Be strong and courageous. Do not be afraid, because I go with you. I have given you confidence to do all things through Christ. I helped David slay Goliath and delivered Daniel from the lions' den. Stand and see the salvation of the Lord. Build your confidence in Me. If your hope and mind are stayed on Me, I will give you the courage to overcome the lions and slay the giants in your life. You can do it, for I am with you!

~God

[Be] confident of this very thing, that he
which hath begun a good work in you will
perform it until the day of Jesus Christ.
PHILIPPIANS 1:6 KJV

Such confidence as this is ours through Christ
before God. Not that we are competent in
ourselves to claim anything for ourselves,
but our competence comes from God.
2 CORINTHIANS 3:4-5 NIV

The Lord shall be your confidence, firm and strong,
and shall keep your foot from being caught
[in a trap or some hidden danger].
PROVERBS 3:26 AMP

Christ Jesus our Lord, in Whom, because of our
faith in Him, we dare to have the boldness (courage
and confidence) of free access (an unreserved
approach to God with freedom and without fear).
EPHESIANS 3:11,12 AMP

"The LORD himself will go before you. He will be
with you; he will not leave you or forget you.
Don't be afraid and don't worry."
DEUTERONOMY 31:8 NCV

O God of our salvation; [You] art the
confidence of all the ends of the earth, and
of them that are afar off upon the sea.
PSALM 65:5 KJV

A *perfect faith would lift us*
absolutely above fear.

CONTENTMENT

My Daughter,

I want you to be content in Me. I am your peace and source of true joy. When you struggle, come to Me and I will still your restless spirit. Allow Me to fill you with the fruit of the Spirit. They are gifts I desire to give you that will bring you great contentment—love, joy, peace, faith. I am all you need in order to live a contented life. When you follow Me, you follow the highest dreams for your life and fulfillment.

~God

Be content with such things as ye have: for he hath
said, I will never leave thee, nor forsake thee.

HEBREWS 13:5 KJV

We know that all things work together for
good to them that love God, to them who
are the called according to his purpose.

ROMANS 8:28 KJV

Godliness with contentment is great gain.

1 TIMOTHY 6:6 NIV

He who dwells in the shelter of the Most High
will rest in the shadow of the Almighty.

PSALM 91:1 NIV

Those who live following their sinful selves think
only about things that their sinful selves want.
But those who live following the Spirit are thinking
about the things the Spirit wants them to do.

ROMANS 8:5 NCV

All the days of the afflicted are evil, but he
who is of a merry heart has a continual feast.

PROVERBS 15:15 NKJV

*Contentment is realizing God has
already given me everything
I need for my present happiness.*

COURAGE

My Daughter,

Take courage because I see the big perspective while your viewpoint of all you are facing is only the size of a keyhole. I know the outcome. When you focus on Me, you will discover a different perspective—a higher perspective. When you are between a rock and a hard place, I will rescue you. Stand still and know that I am God. Ask Me to fill you with a spirit of courage. Be strong and courageous and hope in Me.

~God

Be of good courage, and he shall strengthen your
heart, all ye that hope in the LORD.
PSALM 31:24 KJV

THE LORD IS my light and my salvation; whom shall
I fear? When evil men come to destroy me, they
will stumble and fall! Yes, though a mighty army
marches against me, my heart shall know no fear!
I am confident that God will save me.
PSALM 27:1-3 TLB

I eagerly expect and hope that I will in no way
be ashamed, but will have sufficient courage
so that now as always Christ will be exalted
in my body, whether by life or by death.
PHILIPPIANS 1:20 NIV

"But you, be strong and do not lose courage,
for there is reward for your work."
2 CHRONICLES 15:7 NASB

"Be strong and of good courage, do not fear or be
in dread of them: for it is the LORD your God who
goes with you; he will not fail you or forsake you."
DEUTERONOMY 31:6 RSV

Christ is faithful as a son over God's house.
And we are his house, if we hold on to our courage
and the hope of which we boast.
HEBREWS 3:6 NIV

*Take courage. We walk in the wilderness
today and in the Promised Land tomorrow.*

DELIVERANCE

Beloved,

When you cry for help, I will hear you and deliver you. I am here to rescue you because you know My name. We have a relationship of trust and honor. I will honor you as you honor Me. Your place is in the light of My glory, which is removed from all darkness. Hold on to Me and I will protect you. As I delivered the Israelites from the Egyptians, so will I deliver you from evil and bring you safely into My kingdom.

~Your Deliverer

Because he cleaves to me in love, I will deliver him;
I will protect him, because he knows my name.
When he calls to me, I will answer him; I will be
with him in trouble, I will rescue him and honor him.
PSALM 91:14–15 RSV

He has rescued us out of the darkness and
gloom of Satan's kingdom and brought
us into the kingdom of his dear Son.
COLOSSIANS 1:13 TLB

When the righteous cry for help, the LORD hears,
and delivers them out of all their troubles.
PSALM 34:17 RSV

"The Lord is my rock, my fortress and my deliverer."
2 SAMUEL 22:2 NIV

He who trusts in his own mind is a fool; but
he who walks in wisdom will be delivered.
PROVERBS 28:26 RSV

The Lord will rescue me from every evil attack and
will bring me safely to his heavenly kingdom.
To him be glory for ever and ever. Amen.
2 TIMOTHY 4:18 NIV

*God from the mount of Sinai, whose grey top
Shall tremble, he descending, will himself
In thunder lightning and loud trumpets' sound
Ordain them laws; part such as appertain
To civil justice, part religious rites
Of sacrifice, informing them, by types
And shadows, of that destined seed to bruise
The serpent, by what means he shall achieve
Mankind's deliverance.*

65

ENCOURAGEMENT

My Daughter,

Don't be tempted to give in to discouragement and frustration if the realities of life have thrown your plans into disarray. Look to My Word for encouragement. Take comfort in knowing that I love you and have filled your life with My presence. Submit yourself and your plans to Me. Break forth with singing and shout to the mountaintops with praise. I love you and care for you, so build yourself up through praising Me and watch your joy return. For as you focus on Me, Your discouragement will flee.

~God

Do not gloat over me, my enemy!
Though I have fallen, I will rise. Though I
sit in darkness, the Lord will be my light.

MICAH 7:8 NIV

"Don't lose your courage or be afraid.
Don't panic or be frightened, because the Lord
your God goes with you, to fight for you
against your enemies and to save you."

DEUTERONOMY 20:3-4 NCV

Take delight in the Lord, and he will
give you the desires of your heart.

PSALM 37:4 NRSV

I can do all things in him who strengthens me.

PHILIPPIANS 4:13 RSV

"Be strong and do not let your hands be weak,
for your work shall be rewarded!"

2 CHRONICLES 15:7 NKJV

If we are faithful to the end, trusting God
just as firmly as when we first believed,
we will share in all that belongs to Christ.

HEBREWS 3:14 NLT

Encouragement is oxygen to the soul.

ENDURANCE

Precious One,

Don't give up, but stand firm. I have given you the strength to endure hard times and come through victoriously. Your triumphs don't depend on you alone. Lean on Me and I will help you reach your goal. Your life is in the palm of My hand, and your future is secure with Me. I want to see your dreams realized because I gave many of them to you. Let Me fill you with My Spirit of endurance, for I finished My course, and you will finish yours also.

~Jesus

I have fought the good fight, I have finished the race, I have kept the faith. Finally, there is laid up for me the crown of righteousness, which the Lord, the righteous Judge, will give to me on that Day, and not to me only but also to all who have loved His appearing.

2 TIMOTHY 4:7–8 NKJV

If you suffer for doing good and you endure it, this is commendable before God.

1 PETER 2:20 NIV

Brethren, I do not regard myself as having laid hold of it yet; but one thing I do: forgetting what lies behind and reaching forward to what lies ahead, I press on toward the goal for the prize of the upward call of God in Christ Jesus.

PHILIPPIANS 3:13–14 NASB

After he had patiently endured, he obtained the promise.

HEBREWS 6:15 KJV

Be strong and steady, always enthusiastic about the Lord's work, for you know that nothing you do for the Lord is ever useless.

1 CORINTHIANS 15:58 NLT

Be assured and understand that the trial and proving of your faith bring out endurance and steadfastness and patience.

JAMES 1:3 AMP

*Endurance is the crowning quality,
And patience all the passion of great hearts.*

FAITH

My Daughter,

Faith is the substance of things hoped for and the evidence of things not seen. I challenge you to believe in Me and trust the wonderful promises I have given you. Nurture your faith with My Word and prayer. Let Me give you the strength and power to fulfill your destiny. Let Me be the anchor for your soul, so you won't drift into the sea of doubt and unbelief.

~God

[Jesus] said . . . "Truly I say to you, if you have faith . . . of a mustard seed, you shall say to this mountain, 'Move from here to there,' and it shall move; and nothing shall be impossible to you."
MATTHEW 17:20 NASB

Every child of God can defeat the world, and our faith is what gives us this victory.
1 JOHN 5:4 CEV

"In that day ye shall ask me nothing. Verily, verily, I say unto you, Whatsoever ye shall ask the Father in my name, he will give it you. Hitherto have ye asked nothing in my name: ask, and ye shall receive, that your joy may be full."
JOHN 16:23-24 KJV

Without faith it is impossible to please him: for he that cometh to God must believe that he is, and that he is a rewarder of them that diligently seek him.
HEBREWS 11:6 KJV

I assure you, most solemnly I tell you, if anyone steadfastly believes in Me, he will himself be able to do the things that I do; and he will do even greater things than these, because I go to the Father.
JOHN 14:12 AMP

"Everything is possible for him who believes."
MARK 9:23 NIV

It is the heart which is aware of God, and not reason. That is what faith is: God perceived intuitively by the heart, not by reason.

FAVOR

My Daughter,

You are the apple of My eye. Esteem My favor highly, and know that when you put Me first in everything you do, I will surround you with a shield of favor. I love you and want the very best for you. I desire to bless you at all times and fulfill My wonderful plans for your life. Trust that My power will open doors for you and My hand will be upon your life. The good work I began in you I will bring to completion.

~God

Surely, O Lord, you bless the righteous; you surround them with your favor as with a shield.

PSALM 5:12 NIV

They did not conquer by their own strength and skill, but by your mighty power and because you smiled upon them and favored them.

PSALM 44:3 TLB

May the favor of the Lord our God rest upon us; establish the work of our hands for us— yes, establish the work of our hands.

PSALM 90:17 NIV

In everything you do, put God first, and he will direct you and crown your efforts with success.

PROVERBS 3:6 TLB

"Whoever finds me finds life and receives favor from the Lord."

PROVERBS 8:35 NIV

A *good* name is to be more desired than great wealth, favor is better than silver and gold.

PROVERBS 22:1 NASB

The greatest fault is to be conscious of none.

GRACE

My Daughter,

I am your Light and your Salvation. I long to pour out My grace and glory upon you. I will honor your love and commitment to Me. For you are My treasure and are so precious to Me. My grace and mercy will follow you all the days of your life. Let Me transform you into the person you long to become.

~God

Sin will have no dominion over you, since
you are not under law but under grace.
What then? Should we sin because we are
not under law but under grace? By no means!

ROMANS 6:14-15 NRSV

You know the grace of our Lord Jesus Christ,
that though he was rich, yet for your sakes
he became poor, so that you through
his poverty might become rich.

2 CORINTHIANS 8:9 NIV

"My grace is sufficient for you, for My
strength is made perfect in weakness."

2 CORINTHIANS 12:9 NKJV

"We believe that through the grace
of the Lord Jesus Christ we shall be
saved in the same manner as they."

ACTS 15:11 NKJV

God is able to make all grace abound to you, so
that always having all suffiency in everything,
you may have an abundance for every good deed.

2 CORINTHIANS 9:8 NASB

Where sin increased, grace
increased all the more.

ROMANS 5:20 NIV

*Grace is God himself,
His loving energy at work within His
church and within our souls.*

GUIDANCE

My Daughter,

You have a choice—to lean on your own understanding or to trust Me. I am calling you to walk by faith and not by sight. I have ordered your steps in the way you should go, and I will teach you My ways as I walk with you one step at a time. I will provide the answers you need and show you which way to turn. I am your Guide and Helper. Do not choose to go your own way, for that is the path of destruction. I will lead you on the path of eternal life. Follow Me.

~God

This God is our God for ever and ever;
he will be our guide even to the end.

PSALM 48:14 NIV

The mind of man plans his way,
but the LORD directs his steps.

PROVERBS 16:9 NASB

The steps of a good man are ordered by the LORD:
and he delighteth in his way.

PSALM 37:23 KJV

I will instruct you (says the Lord) and guide you
along the best pathway for your life; I will
advise you and watch your progress.

PSALM 32:8 TLB

Trust in the LORD with all thine heart; and lean not
unto thine own understanding. In all thy ways
acknowledge him, and he shall direct thy paths.

PROVERBS 3:5-6 KJV

Thy word is a lamp unto my feet,
and a light unto my path.

PSALM 119:105 KJV

*God made the moon as well as the sun; and
when He does not see fit to grant us the
sunlight, He means us
to guide our steps by moonlight.*

 # HAPPINESS

My Daughter,

Everlasting happiness comes from your relationship with Me. As you spend time with Me, your heart will be gladdened and you will be happy from the inside out. I will fill your day with small pleasures that bring you joy. Pause and look at the little gifts I give you to bring a smile to your heart. Allow My goodness and My presence to bring laughter and fulfillment to your daily life.

~God

A glad heart makes a cheerful countenance.

PROVERBS 15:13 AMP

To the man who pleases him God gives
wisdom and knowledge and joy.

ECCLESIASTES 2:26 RSV

You will teach me how to live a holy life.
Being with you will fill me with joy; at
your right hand I will find pleasure forever.

PSALM 16:11 NCV

"The one whom God corrects is happy, so do
not hate being corrected by the Almighty."

JOB 5:17 NCV

Happy are the people whose God is the LORD.

PSALM 144:15 NRSV

Happy are those who are helped by the God
of Jacob. Their hope is in the LORD their God.

PSALM 146:5 NCV

*Happiness is not a state to arrive at,
but a manner of traveling.*

HEALTH & HEALING

My Daughter,

My desire is for you to live in health
all the days of your life. Bring Me your
pain, sorrow, and grief and I will give
you joy and health. Hold on to Me
because I am your strength. I want you
to live out all the days of your life and
fulfill every plan I have set before you.
I am the Lord who heals you.

~God

Yes, I will bless the Lord and not forget
the glorious things he does for me.
He forgives all my sins. He heals me.

PSALM 103:2-3 TLB

O Lord my God, I called out to you
for help and you healed me.

PSALM 30:2 NIV

"I will restore you to health and I will heal you
of your wounds," declares the LORD.

JEREMIAH 30:17 NASB

Surely He has borne our griefs and carried our
sorrows; yet we esteemed Him stricken, smitten
by God, and afflicted. But He was wounded
for our transgressions, He was bruised for our
iniquities; the chastisement for our peace was
upon Him, and by His stripes we are healed.

ISAIAH 53:4-5 NKJV

"I am the LORD, who heals you."

EXODUS 15:26 NIV

"You who fear my name, the Sun of Righteousness
will rise with healing in his wings. And you
will go free, leaping with joy like calves let out to
pasture."

MALACHI 4:2 TLB

℘

He who formed our frame
Made man a perfect whole
And made the body's health
Depend upon the soul.

HOPE

My Daughter,

Hope is an earnest expectation—so
have an earnest expectation of Me.
Believe I love you and want the very best
for you. Be encouraged in My Word and
know that I desire to see you achieve
great things in your life. Experience joy
in My presence and encourage your
heart by knowing that I desire to see you
accomplish your purpose. Hang your
hope on Me and trust that I will fulfill
My plans for you.

~God

I pray also that the eyes of your heart may be
enlightened in order that you may know the hope
to which [God] has called you, the riches of
his glorious inheritance in the saints, and his
incomparably great power for us who believe.
EPHESIANS 1:18-19 NIV

Be of good courage, and he shall strengthen
your heart, all ye that hope in the LORD.
PSALM 31:24 KJV

Praise God, the Father of our Lord Jesus Christ.
God is so good, and by raising Jesus from death,
he has given us new life and a hope that lives on.
1 PETER 1:3 CEV

May the God of hope fill you with all joy and
peace in believing, so that you may abound
in hope by the power of the Holy Spirit.
ROMANS 15:13 NASB

O Lord, you alone are my hope;
I've trusted you from childhood.
PSALM 71:5 TLB

Everything that was written in the past
was written to teach us, so that through
endurance and the encouragement of
the Scriptures we might have hope.
ROMANS 15:4 NIV

Hope *is an adventure, a going forward—a*
confident search for a rewarding life.

PATIENCE

My Daughter,

I know you find it difficult at times to remain patient. Look at patience as if you were a farmer waiting for a field to grow. Before he is able to harvest his reward, he must diligently wait for the right season. Allow Me to work out things for good in your life, and give Me time to do it. Cast your anxieties on Me and rest in My love. You will have your answers in due season, because patience will bring reward to your life.

~God

My brethren, count it all joy when you fall
into various trials, knowing that the testing
of your faith produces patience. But let
patience have its perfect work, that you may
be perfect and complete, lacking nothing.

JAMES 1:2-4 NKJV

You need to keep on patiently doing
God's will if you want him to do
for you all that he has promised.

HEBREWS 10:36 TLB

I waited patiently for the LORD to help me,
and he turned to me and heard my cry.

PSALM 40:1 NLT

Be humble and gentle. Be patient with
each other, making allowance for each
other's faults because of your love.

EPHESIANS 4:2 TLB

Be like those who through faith and patience
will receive what God has promised.

HEBREWS 6:12 NCV

Be patient and stand firm, because
the Lord's coming is near.

JAMES 5:8 NIV

*Never think that God's delays are God's
denials. Hold on; hold fast; hold out.
Patience is genius.*

PEACE

My Daughter,

Great is the peace and undisturbed composure of these who trust in Me. I desire to give you peace like a river that flows on and on. Even when it seems as if you are experiencing a drought in your life, when you feel parched by life's trials, the river of life flows from My throne to your heart. Like the water flows through the land providing water for life, so My life-giving peace flows to you. You are a tree planted by My rivers of living water. Stay close to the peaceful waters of My Spirit.

~God

Consider the blameless, observe the upright;
there is a future for the man of peace.

PSALM 37:37 NIV

The peace of God, which passeth all
understanding, shall keep your hearts
and minds through Christ Jesus.

PHILIPPIANS 4:7 KJV

He will keep in perfect peace all those who trust
in him, whose thoughts turn often to the Lord!

ISAIAH 26:3 TLB

Therefore, since we have been justified
through faith, we have peace with
God through our Lord Jesus Christ.

ROMANS 5:1 NIV

"Blessed are the peacemakers,
for they shall be called sons of God."

MATTHEW 5:9 NKJV

"I am leaving you with a gift—peace of mind
and heart. And the peace I give isn't
like the peace the world gives.
So don't be troubled or afraid."

JOHN 14:27 NLT

*Peace is the deliberate adjustment of
my life to the will of God.*

PERSEVERANCE

My Daughter,

Stand fast and hold tightly to Me. I love you and have given you everlasting consolation and good hope through grace. Comfort your heart for I have established you in every good word and work. I hear your prayers and listen to the words that you speak. I will uphold your soul. Hold on to all I have promised, and you will see My faithfulness and fruit in your life.

~God

You need to persevere so that when
you have done the will of God, you
will receive what he has promised.

HEBREWS 10:36 NIV

Blessed is the man who endures trial, for when he
has stood the test he will receive the crown of life
which God has promised to those who love him.

JAMES 1:12 RSV

We also exult in our tribulations, knowing
that tribulation brings about perseverance;
and perseverance, proven character;
and proven character, hope.

ROMANS 5:3-4 NASB

Consider it pure joy, my brothers, whenever you
face trials of many kinds, because you know that
the testing of your faith develops perseverance.
Perseverance must finish its work so that you may
be mature and complete, not lacking anything.

JAMES 1:2-4 NIV

He will keep you strong to the end, so that you will
be blameless on the day of our Lord Jesus Christ.

1 CORINTHIANS 1:8 NIV

We are hard pressed on every side, but not crushed;
perplexed, but not in despair; persecuted, but not
abandoned; struck down, but not destroyed.

2 CORINTHIANS 4:8-9 NIV

*Few things are impossible
to diligence and skill.*

 # PROSPERITY

My Daughter,

I take pleasure in your prosperity and I truly enjoy meeting your needs. I desire to bless you with My abundance so that you can be a blessing to others and confirm My covenant with you. I want to give you good gifts—it thrills Me most when you acknowledge Me as your perfect gift and embrace My love. For these are the gifts that endure.

~God

Seek ye first the kingdom of God,
and his righteousness; and all these
things shall be added unto you.
MATTHEW 6:33 KJV

If they obey and serve him, they will spend the rest of
their days in prosperity and their years in contentment.
JOB 36:11 NIV

Every one that hath forsaken houses, or brethren,
or sisters, or father, or mother, or wife, or children,
or lands, for my name's sake, shall receive an
hundredfold, and shall inherit everlasting life.
MATTHEW 19:29 KJV

"If you carefully obey the rules and regulations which
he gave to Israel through Moses, you will prosper.
Be strong and courageous, fearless and enthusiastic!"
1 CHRONICLES 22:13 TLB

Carefully follow the terms of this covenant,
so that you may prosper in everything you do.
DEUTERONOMY 29:9 NIV

Let them shout for joy and rejoice, who favor
my vindication; and let them say continually,
"The LORD be magnified, Who delights
in the prosperity of His servant."
PSALM 35:27 NASB

*Everything we are given and everything we
are deprived of is nothing but a finger
pointing out the direction of God's hidden
promise, which we shall taste in full.*

PROTECTION

My Daughter,

Come and live with Me in the secret place, and I will shadow you with My wings. I am your refuge and fortress: trust Me. I will deliver you. My truth is your shield. You have no reason to fear or become terrified. While a thousand fall at your side, and ten thousand at your right hand, it won't come near you. Only with your eyes will you see the reward of the wicked because you set your love on Me. I have given My angels charge over you to keep you safe. With long life I satisfy you and show you My salvation.

~God

The Angel of the Lord guards and
rescues all who reverence him.

PSALM 34:7 TLB

Fear not, for I am with you, be not dismayed, for I
am your God; I will strengthen you, I will help you,
I will uphold you with my victorious right hand.

ISAIAH 41:10 RSV

The Lord is faithful, and He will strengthen
and protect you from the evil one.

2 THESSALONIANS 3:3 NASB

The Lord is a strong fortress.
The godly run to him and are safe.

PROVERBS 18:10 TLB

The LORD shall preserve you from all evil;
He shall preserve your soul. The LORD shall
preserve your going out and your coming in
from this time forth, and even forevermore.

PSALM 121:7-8 NKJV

He that dwelleth in the secret place of the most
High shall abide under the shadow of the Almighty.
I will say of the LORD, He is my refuge and my
fortress: my God; in him will I trust.

PSALM 91:1-2 KJV

God incarnate is the end of fear;
and the heart that realizes
that he is in the midst . . .
will be quiet in the midst of alarm.

REDEMPTION

My Daughter,

I bought you with a precious price and consider you worth the sacrifice. Your salvation is secure through the gift Jesus made in His death, burial, and resurrection. You are pardoned and your sin is no longer a memory but forgotten—washed away in the flow of the blood of Jesus. I love you.

~God

When the fullness of the time came, God sent forth
His Son, born of a woman, born under the Law, so
that He might redeem those who were under the
Law, that we might receive the adoption as sons.

GALATIANS 4:4-5 NASB

As for those who serve the Lord,
he will redeem them; everyone who
takes refuge in him will be freely pardoned.

PSALM 34:22 TLB

He did not enter by means of . . . goats and calves;
but he entered the Most Holy Place once for all by
his own blood, having obtained eternal redemption.

HEBREWS 9:12 NIV

All have sinned, and come short of the glory
of God; being justified freely by his grace
through the redemption that is in Christ Jesus.

ROMANS 3:23-24 KJV

He has rescued us from the power of darkness and
transferred us into the kingdom of his beloved Son, in
whom we have redemption, the forgiveness of sins.

COLOSSIANS 1:13-14 NRSV

In him we have redemption through his blood,
the forgiveness of sins, in accordance with
the riches of God's grace that he lavished
on us with all wisdom and understanding.

EPHESIANS 1:7-8 NIV

God is my strong salvation,
What foe have I to fear?
In darkness and temptation,
My light, my help is near.

RESTORATION

My Daughter,

I am your Restorer. In My lovingkindness
I will restore to you the years that have
been wasted or eaten away by the evil
one. I will strengthen you and raise
you up. I will forgive your sins and
restore to you the joy of My salvation. I
will satisfy you with My presence and
fill you with My Spirit.

                    ~Your Restorer

Turn to God! Give up your sins, and you will
be forgiven. Then that time will come when
the Lord will give you fresh strength.

ACTS 3:19-20 CEV

The God of all grace, who called you to his
eternal glory in Christ, after you have suffered
a little while, will himself restore you and
make you strong, firm and steadfast.

1 PETER 5:10 NIV

He restores my soul.

PSALM 23:3 NKJV

Restore to me again the joy of your salvation,
and make me willing to obey you.

PSALM 51:12 TLB

Though you have made me see troubles, many
and bitter, you will restore my life again; from the
depths of the earth you will again bring me up.

PSALM 71:20 NIV

Be made new in the attitude of your minds;
and . . . put on the new self, created to be
like God in true righteousness and holiness.

EPHESIANS 4:23-24 NIV

*C*onfession, *which means to agree with God
regarding our sin, restores our fellowship.*

SELF-CONTROL

My Daughter,

I have given you the spirit of power so that you can direct your steps in the path of righteousness. Your body is the temple of My Spirit, so lend yourself to the things that please Me. Don't allow your impulses or your emotions to rule your life, but rather give yourself over to Me and let My Spirit empower you to live a life for Me.

~God

Stop depriving one another, except by agreement
for a time, so that you may devote yourselves to
prayer, and come together again so that Satan will
not tempt you because of your lack of self-control.
1 CORINTHIANS 7:5 NASB

Above all else, guard your heart,
for it affects everything you do.
PROVERBS 4:23 NLT

Knowing God leads to self-control.
Self-control leads to patient endurance,
and patient endurance leads to godliness.
2 PETER 1:6 NLT

He who guards his mouth and his tongue
keeps himself from troubles.
PROVERBS 21:23 AMP

Every man that striveth for the mastery is
temperate in all things. Now they do it to obtain
a corruptible crown; but we an incorruptible.
1 CORINTHIANS 9:25 KJV

Brothers and sisters, you have no obligation
whatsoever to do what your sinful nature urges you
to do. For if you keep on following it, you will
perish. But if through the power of the Holy Spirit
you turn from it and its evil deeds, you will live.
ROMANS 8:12–13 NLT

*Self-control is the ability to keep cool while
someone is making it hot for you.*

STABILITY

My Daughter,

In times of trouble and chaos, depend on Me. I will quiet your fears and proclaim peace to the storms in your life. Meditate on My faithfulness, for I will never leave you or forsake you. When you call to Me, I will answer you. No matter how rough the water, I will steady your ship. Keep your eyes on Me, for I will always be with you. I am the anchor of your soul.

~God

Wisdom and knowledge will be the stability
of your times, and the strength of salvation;
the fear of the LORD *is* His treasure.

ISAIAH 33:6 NKJV

If we are faithful to the end, trusting God just
as we did when we first became Christians,
we will share in all that belongs to Christ.

HEBREWS 3:14 TLB

He will not fear evil tidings; his heart
is steadfast, trusting in the LORD.

PSALM 112:7 NASB

Be steadfast, immovable, always abounding
in the work of the Lord, knowing that
your labor is not in vain in the Lord.

1 CORINTHIANS 15:58 NKJV

He is the living God, and stedfast for ever,
and his kingdom that which shall not be destroyed;
and his dominion shall be even unto the end.

DANIEL 6:26 ASV

"Grass withers and flowers fade, but the
word of our God endures forever."

ISAIAH 40:8 TEV

*S*tability is found in
God's unfailing love.

STRENGTH

My Daughter,

I created you to need Me. You have little strength apart from Me. Yet when you recognize your weakness and humbly seek My face, I The Lord Omnipotent, become your strength. Then you will find the grace and strength to proclaim, "The Lord is the strength of my life". I long to show myself strong on your behalf. Will you entrust yourself to Me and let Me strengthen the knees that are feeble?

~God

He will give his people strength.
He will bless them with peace.

PSALM 29:11 TLB

I can do everything through him
who gives me strength.

PHILIPPIANS 4:13 NIV

He giveth power to the faint; and to them
that have no might he increaseth strength.

ISAIAH 40:29 KJV

They that wait upon the Lord shall renew their
strength. They shall mount up with wings
like eagles; they shall run and not be weary;
they shall walk and not faint.

ISAIAH 40:31 TLB

"My grace is sufficient for you, for My
strength is made perfect in weakness."

2 CORINTHIANS 12:9 NKJV

My flesh and my heart fail; but God is the
strength of my heart and my portion forever.

PSALM 73:26 NKJV

*The weaker we feel, the harder we
lean on God. And the harder
we lean, the stronger we grow.*

SUCCESS

My Daughter,

I have plans for your life that will lead you down the road of true success, but My eternal plans require external perspective. Don't become discouraged when you stumble and fall, for I have called and anointed you. I will accompany you for the entire journey. I desire to see you as the head and not the tail. So stay close to Me, and allow Me to work in your life. Follow My instructions and you will achieve everlasting success.

~God

The Lord will grant you abundant prosperity—in the fruit of your womb, the young of your livestock and the crops of your ground—in the land he swore to your forefathers to give you. The Lord will open the heavens, the storehouse of his bounty, to send rain on your land in season and to bless all the work of your hands. You will lend to many nations but will borrow from none.

DEUTERONOMY 28:11–12 NIV

True humility and respect for the Lord lead
a man to riches, honor and long life.

PROVERBS 22:4 TLB

This book of the law shall not depart out of your mouth, but you shall meditate on it day and night, that you may be careful to do according to all that is written in it; for then you shall make your way prosperous, and then you shall have good success.

JOSHUA 1:8 RSV

It is not that we think we can do anything
of lasting value by ourselves. Our only
power and success come from God.

2 CORINTHIANS 3:5 NLT

Surely I know the plans I have for you, says the
Lord, plans for your welfare and not for harm,
to give you a future with hope.

JEREMIAH 29:11 NRSV

He had great success in everything he did because
the Lord was with him.

1 SAMUEL 18:14 NCV

*He has achieved success who has lived well,
laughed often, and loved much.*

UNDERSTANDING

My Daughter,

It is hard for you to understand life without My illumination upon your heart and mind. Will you make your ear attentive to My wisdom? Will you incline your heart to My understanding? Ask Me to give you understanding so that you can know Me and walk in My ways. And also so you can be a blessing to those around you. I will surely answer your heart's cry, for I delight in you.

~God

Yes, if you want better insight and discernment,
and are searching for them as you would for
lost money or hidden treasure, then wisdom
will be given you, and knowledge of God himself;
you will soon learn the importance of reverence
for the Lord and of trusting him. For the
Lord grants wisdom! His every word is a
treasure of knowledge and understanding.

PROVERBS 2:3-6 TLB

The entrance of Your words gives light;
it gives understanding to the simple.

PSALM 119:130 NKJV

Trust in the LORD with all thine heart; and
lean not unto thine own understanding.

PROVERBS 3:5 KJV

Good understanding produces favor.

PROVERBS 13:15 NASB

Discretion will guard you,
understanding will watch over you,
to deliver you from the way of evil,
from the man who speaks perverse things.

PROVERBS 2:11-12 NASB

Call to Me and I will answer you, and I will tell you
great and mighty things, which you do not know.

JEREMIAH 33:3 NASB

It is a luxury to be understood.

WISDOM

My Daughter,

If you lack wisdom, you need only to ask Me and I will give it to you, for I give good gifts to My children. Wisdom is the principle thing, so get wisdom. It is more valuable than money, status, fame, or fortune. So let your heart retain My words, for they contain the seeds of supernatural wisdom that will be planted in your heart.

~God

There shall be stability in your times,
an abundance of salvation, wisdom, and
knowledge; the reverent fear and worship
of the Lord is your treasure and His.

ISAIAH 33:6 AMP

In Him we have redemption through his blood,
for the forgiveness of sins, in accordance with
the riches of God's grace that He lavished
on us with all wisdom and understanding

EPHESIANS 1:7-8 NIV

If you want to know what God wants you to do,
ask him, and he will gladly tell you, for he
is always ready to give a bountiful supply of
wisdom to all who ask him; he will not resent it.

JAMES 1:5 TLB

If any of you needs wisdom, you should ask
God for it. He is generous and enjoys giving
to all people, so he will give you wisdom.

JAMES 1:5 NCV

To the man who pleases him, God gives
wisdom, knowledge and happiness.

ECCLESIASTES 2:26 NIV

The knowledge of the Holy One is understanding.
For by me your days will be multiplied,
and years of life will be added to you.

PROVERBS 9:10-11 NASB

*W*isdom is seeing life from
God's perspective.

GOD'S PROMISES
WHEN
I FEEL . . .

 ANGRY

My Daughter,

I am here to heal your emotions. Give Me your anger and draw strength from Me. Just as I offer forgiveness, you can choose to forgive those who have angered you. I will make a way for healing and restoration if you will open the door for Me in this situation. Follow My lead and watch loving-kindness flow from your heart to the one who has hurt you. I have a higher perspective and I will show you how to forgive if you will ask Me. Let go and allow Me to fill you with my peace. I love you.

~God

He that is slow to anger is better than the mighty;
and he that ruleth his spirit than he that taketh a city.
PROVERBS 16:32 KJV

Good sense makes a man slow to anger,
and it is his glory to overlook an offense.
PROVERBS 19:11 RSV

A wise man controls his temper.
He knows that anger causes mistakes.
PROVERBS 14:29 TLB

Those who control their anger have great
understanding; those with a hasty temper will
make mistakes.
PROVERBS 14:29 NLT

Do everything without complaining or arguing.
Then you will be innocent and without any wrong.
You will be God's children without fault. But you are
living with crooked and mean people all around you,
among whom you shine like stars in the dark world.
PHILIPPIANS 2:14-15 NCV

"I'm challenging that. I'm telling you to love your
enemies. Let them bring out the best in you, not the
worst. When someone gives you a hard time, respond
with the energies of prayer, for then you are working
out of your true selves, your God-created selves. This
is what God does. He gives his best—the sun to warm
and the rain to nourish—to everyone, regardless: the
good and bad, the nice and nasty."
MATTHEW 5:44-45 THE MESSAGE

*Anger is quieted by a gentle word just
as fire is quenched by water.*

ANXIOUS

My Daughter,

Pursue Me and don't fuss about what's on the table at mealtimes or whether the clothes in your closet are in fashion. There is far more to your life than the food you put in your stomach and more to your appearance than the clothes you hang on your body. If I give much attention to the appearance of wildflowers, I will attend to you, take pride in you, and do the best for you. Focus your attention on Me and trust My provisions in your life. Don't worry about missing out. You'll find that all of your everyday concerns will be taken care of. Give your entire attention to what I'm doing right now, and don't worry about what may or may not happen tomorrow. I'll help you when that time comes. Don't let anxiety and fear rob you of living and enjoying today. It is My gift to you.

~God

Do not be anxious about anything,
but in everything, by prayer and petition,
with thanksgiving, present your requests to God.
And the peace of God, which transcends all
understanding, will guard your hearts
and your minds in Christ Jesus.

PHILIPPIANS 4:6–7 NIV

For I, the LORD your God, hold your right hand;
it is I who say to you, "Fear not, I will help you."

ISAIAH 41:13 RSV

These things I have spoken unto you, that
in me ye might have peace. In the world ye
shall have tribulation: but be of good cheer;
I have overcome the world.

JOHN 16:33 KJV

Therefore humble yourselves under the mighty hand
of God, that He may exalt you in due time, casting
all your care upon Him, for He cares for you.

1 PETER 5:6–7 NKJV

Cast thy burden upon the LORD,
and he shall sustain thee.

PSALM 55:22 KJV

"Come to me, all you who are weary and
burdened, and I will give you rest."

MATTHEW 11:28 NIV

I*t ain't no use putting up your
umbrella till it rains.*

CONFUSED

My Daughter,

I am not the author of confusion.
Rather, I am the Shepherd of your soul.
I desire to lead you, My sheep, into the
green pastures of peace and confidence.
When you feel confused, come to Me
and I will settle your mind until you
can hear Me clearly again. I can
replace uncertainty with wisdom,
shine the light of truth on the
situations in your life, and set you free
to make good choices.

~God

If you want to know what God wants you to do,
ask him, and he will gladly tell you, for he is
always ready to give a bountiful supply of wisdom
to all who ask him; he will not resent it.
JAMES 1:5 TLB

Trust the Lord with all your heart, and don't depend
on your own understanding. Remember the Lord
in all you do, and he will give you success.
PROVERBS 3:5-6 NCV

"Instead of your shame you shall have double
honor, and instead of confusion they shall rejoice
in their portion. Therefore in their land they shall
possess double; everlasting joy shall be theirs.
For I, the Lord, love justice; I hate robbery for
burnt offering; I will direct their work in truth."
ISAIAH 61:7-8 NKJV

The fear of man bringeth a snare: but whoso
putteth his trust in the LORD shall be safe.
PROVERBS 29:25 KJV

Your ears will hear a word behind you,
"This is the way, walk in it," whenever
you turn to the right or to the left.
ISAIAH 30:21 NASB

In You, O Lord, do I put my trust and confidently take
refuge; let me never be put to shame or confusion!
PSALM 71:1 AMP

*T*ruth frees you from confusion.

DISAPPOINTED

My Daughter,

I know the disappointments of your heart and desire to be your hope when you feel as if life has let you down. Trust Me in the midst of your disappointment and believe that I am always looking out for what's best for you. Remember, you have not yet reached the end of the story. So don't be discouraged . . . . I am still at work creating a beautiful tapestry in your life.

~God

That is why we never give up. Though our bodies
are dying, our spirits are being renewed every day.

2 CORINTHIANS 4:16 NLT

The Scriptures tell us that no one who believes
in Christ will ever be disappointed.

ROMANS 10:11 TLB

[Be] confident of this very thing, that
He who has begun a good work in you will
complete it until the day of Jesus Christ.

PHILIPPIANS 1:6 NKJV

As the Scriptures express it, "See, I am sending
Christ to be the carefully chosen, precious
Cornerstone of my church, and I will never
disappoint those who trust in him."

1 PETER 2:6 TLB

Why are you cast down, O my soul? And why are
you disquieted within me? Hope in God, for I shall
yet praise Him for the help of His countenance.

PSALM 42:5 NKJV

This expectation will not disappoint us.
For we know how dearly God loves us,
because he has given us the Holy Spirit
to fill our hearts with his love.

ROMANS 5:5 NLT

*Look upon your chastenings as God's
chariots sent to carry your soul into
the high places of achievement.*

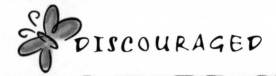

DISCOURAGED

My Daughter,

I believe in you. I can see the whole picture while you can see only what is right before you. Lift your head and look to Me. I have an eternal perspective on this temporary situation in your life. The plans I have for you far exceed what you have imagined. I believe in you, so take courage to believe in yourself and in the dreams I have placed in your heart.

~God

O my soul, why be so gloomy and discouraged?
Trust in God! I shall again praise him for
his wondrous help; he will make me
smile again, for he is my God!

PSALM 43:5 TLB

Christ, God's faithful Son, is in complete charge of
God's house. And we Christians are God's house—
he lives in us!—if we keep up our courage firm to
the end, and our joy and our trust in the Lord.

HEBREWS 3:6 TLB

I waited patiently and expectantly for the Lord;
and He inclined to me and heard my cry.

PSALM 40:1 AMP

"Keep up the good work and don't get
discouraged, for you will be rewarded."

2 CHRONICLES 15:7 TLB

Though he stumble, he will not fall,
for the Lord upholds him with his hand.

PSALM 37:24 NIV

Look, the Lord your God has set the land
before you; go up and possess it, as the
Lord God of your fathers has spoken to you;
do not fear or be discouraged.

DEUTERONOMY 1:21 NKJV

*Never doubt in dark what God
told you in the light.*

FEARFUL

My Daughter,

Do not be afraid, because I am with you. Do not give in to the spirit of fear that is so prevalent in the world. Instead, trust Me to love you and care for you daily. You can walk confidently through the battles of life with Me as your powerful ally. Remember My goodness to you in the past, and choose to trust that I will provide for you now . . . and forever.

~God

Fear thou not; for I am with thee: be not dismayed;
for I am thy God: I will strengthen thee;
yea, I will help thee; yea, I will uphold thee
with the right hand of my righteousness.
ISAIAH 41:10 KJV

God did not give us a spirit of timidity, but a
spirit of power, of love and of self-discipline.
2 TIMOTHY 1:7 NIV

My flesh and my heart may fail, but God is the Rock
and firm Strength of my heart and my Portion forever.
PSALM 73:26 AMP

Even though I walk through the valley of the
shadow of death, I will fear no evil, for you are
with me; your rod and your staff, they comfort me.
PSALM 23:4 NIV

"Do not fear, for those who are with us are
more than those who are with them."
2 KINGS 6:16 NASB

There is no fear in love. But perfect love drives out
fear, because fear has to do with punishment.
The one who fears is not made perfect in love.
1 JOHN 4:18 NIV

*Fear imprisons, faith liberates; fear
paralyzes, faith empowers; fear disheartens,
faith encourages; fear sickens, faith heals; fear
makes useless, faith makes serviceable—and,
most of all, fear puts hopelessness at the heart
of life, while faith rejoices in its God.*

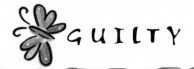 # GUILTY

My Daughter,

My Son, Jesus, bore your guilt on the cross when He paid for your sins. You are forgiven and your sins are remembered no more. The hidden sins that darkened your heart are gone, and I have given you a clean heart. You are a new creature in Christ, who will not find condemnation before Me. Please accept My love and grace. See yourself as I do and enter into the freedom of your redemption.

~God

Now there is no condemnation for
those who belong to Christ Jesus.

ROMANS 8:1 NLT

Create in me a clean heart, O God,
And renew a steadfast spirit within me.

PSALM 51:10 NASB

You, O Lord, keep my lamp burning;
my God turns my darkness into light.

PSALM 18:28 NIV

"They sinned against me, but I will wash away
that sin. They did evil and turned away
from me, but I will forgive them."

JEREMIAH 33:8 NCV

Consecrate yourselves therefore, and be holy; for I
am the Lord your God. Keep my statutes, and
observe them; I am the Lord; I sanctify you.

LEVITICUS 20:7-8 NRSV

Christ also loved the church and gave Himself for
her, that He might sanctify and cleanse her with
the washing of water by the word, that He might
present her to Himself a glorious church, not
having spot or wrinkle or any such thing, but that
she should be holy and without blemish.

EPHESIANS 5:25-27 NKJV

*Guilt is the most destructive of all emotions.
It mourns what has been while playing no
part in what may be, now or in the future.*

JEALOUS

My Daughter,

Sometimes it is not so much that you envy what others have, but rather what they represent—all the things the world wants you to be. I made you in My image and likeness, so jealousy often signals that you are worshipping something other than Me. Take your eyes off them and look to Me. In My eyes you are growing and are complete in Christ, so see yourself through My eyes. I will help you cleanse your thoughts, renew your heart, and restore a right focus in your life. Allow Me to be the center of your life.

~God

A relaxed attitude lengthens life;
jealousy rots it away.

PROVERBS 14:30 NLT

"I will feast the soul of the priests with
abundance, and my people shall be satisfied
with my goodness, says the LORD."

JEREMIAH 31:14 RSV

Don't envy sinners, but always respect the Lord.
Then you will have hope for the future,
and your wishes will come true.

PROVERBS 23:17-18 NCV

Make sure that your character is free from the love
of money, being content with what you have; for
He Himself has said, "I WILL NEVER DESERT YOU,
NOR WILL I EVER FORSAKE YOU."

HEBREWS 13:5 NASB

Be still before the Lord and wait patiently for him;
do not fret when men succeed in their ways,
when they carry out their wicked schemes. . . .
For evil men will be cut off, but those
who hope in the Lord will inherit the land.

PSALM 37:7, 9 NIV

He satisfies me with good things and
makes me young again, like the eagle.

PSALM 103:5 NCV

*Jealousy contains more of
self-love than of love.*

LONELY

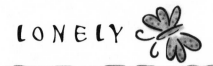

My Daughter,

When you feel alone in the world,
remember that I am with you and I
love you. I will comfort you in every
circumstance, as you are My beloved
child. Though others reject you, I will
not reject you. I accept you and will
not abandon you. Allow the lonely
times you feel to become gentle
reminders to come near to Me and
experience My presence in your life.

~God

"Behold, I am with you and will keep you
wherever you go, and will bring you back
to this land; for I will not leave you until I have
done that of which I have spoken to you."

GENESIS 28:15 RSV

Even if my father and mother abandon me,
the LORD will hold me close.

PSALM 27:10 NLT

God makes a home for the lonely;
He leads out the prisoners into prosperity,
Only the rebellious dwell in a parched land.

PSALM 68:6 NASB

I am persuaded that neither . . . height
nor depth, nor any other created things,
shall be able to separate us from the love
of God which is in Christ Jesus our Lord.

ROMANS 8:38-39 NKJV

The eternal God is thy refuge, and
underneath are the everlasting arms.

DEUTERONOMY 33:27 KJV

You are my hiding place; you protect me
from trouble. You surround me
with songs of victory.

PSALM 32:7 NLT

*Loneliness is the first thing that God's eye
nam'd not good.*

PERSECUTED

My Daughter,

When you are persecuted for My name, you are in good company. Whatever others have done to you, they have also done to Me. Forgive them, turn your hurts over to Me, and allow Me to take care of you. Entrust the outcome to Me, for I judge justly. In the end, your integrity shall uphold you. You are the apple of My eye, so rejoice in Me, for My glory rests upon you.

~God

"Blessed are those who have been persecuted
for the sake of righteousness, for theirs is
the kingdom of heaven. Blessed are you when
people insult you and persecute you, and falsely
say all kinds of evil against you because of Me."

MATTHEW 5:10-11 NASB

We have this treasure in earthen vessels, so that the
surpassing greatness of the power will be of God and not
from ourselves; we are afflicted in every way, but not
crushed; perplexed, but not despairing; persecuted, but
not forsaken; struck down, but not destroyed; always
carrying about in the body the dying of Jesus, so that
the life of Jesus also may be manifested in our body.

2 CORINTHIANS 4:7-10 NASB

Let all who take refuge in you be glad; let them ever
sing for joy. Spread your protection over them, that
those who love your name may rejoice in you.
For surely, O Lord, you bless the righteous; you
surround them with your favor as with a shield.

PSALM 5:11-12 NIV

I say unto you, Love your enemies, bless them that
curse you, do good to them that hate you, and pray for
them which despitefully use you, and persecute you.

MATTHEW 5:44 KJV

I will restore health to you, and I will heal your
wounds, says the Lord, because they have called
you an outcast, saying, This is Zion, whom no one
seeks after and for whom no one cares!

JEREMIAH 30:17 AMP

Bless those who persecute you [who are cruel in their
attitude toward you]; bless and do not curse them.

ROMANS 12:14 AMP

*Wherever you see persecution, there is more than a
probability that truth is on the persecuted side.*

131

PRIDEFUL

My Daughter,

Do not think more highly of yourself
than you ought, but remember that
everything good in you and all the
blessings you have are gifts from Me.
The world will tell you that you must
fight for what is yours and trample
others on your way to the top. That is
not My way. Listen to My wisdom and
choose the path of humility. The first
shall be last and the last shall be first.
Trust Me to make a way for you rather
than trying to make a way for yourself.
Enjoy the privileges of a humble child
loved by your adoring Father, and treat
others as I treat you.

~God

"He who humbles himself will be exalted."
LUKE 18:14 NKJV

A humble spirit will obtain honor.
PROVERBS 29:23 NASB

When swelling and pride come, then emptiness and shame come also.
PROVERBS 11:2 AMP

Whoever becomes simple and elemental again, like this child, will rank high in God's kingdom.
MATTHEW 18:4 THE MESSAGE

To the faithful you show yourself faithful, to the blameless you show yourself blameless, to the pure you show yourself pure, but to the crooked you show yourself shrewd. You save the humble, but your eyes are on the haughty to bring them low.
2 SAMUEL 22:26–28 NIV

Through the grace given to me I say to everyone among you not to think more highly of himself than he ought to think; but to think so as to have sound judgment, as God has allotted to each a measure of faith.
ROMANS 12:3 NASB

Our intellect and other gifts have been given to be used for God's greater glory, but sometimes they become the very god for us. That is the saddest part: we are losing our balance when this happens. We must free ourselves to be filled by God. Even God cannot fill what is full.

STRESSED

My Daughter,

Don't fill your plate so full. You don't have to please everyone. It's okay to say no. You can find the quietness and peace you need by trusting in Me and letting Me care for you. Choose the most treasured things to fill your plate, and then take time to enjoy them. Live your life with an eternal rhythm instead of living by the clock. Abide in Me and I'll give you My peace. Remember, unless the Lord build the house, they labor in vain who build it.

~God

"Come to Me, all you who labor and are heavy laden, and I will give you rest."

MATTHEW 11:28 NKJV

Cast your burden upon the LORD and He will sustain you; He will never allow the righteous to be shaken.

PSALM 55:22 NASB

You will keep in perfect peace him whose mind is steadfast, because he trusts in you. Trust in the Lord forever, for the Lord, the Lord, is the Rock eternal.

ISAIAH 26:3-4 NIV

Consider the blameless, observe the upright; there is a future for the man of peace.

PSALM 37:37 NIV

The peace of God, which passeth all understanding, shall keep your hearts and minds through Christ Jesus.

PHILIPPIANS 4:7 KJV

Those who trust in, lean on, and confidently hope in the Lord are like Mount Zion, which cannot be moved but abides and stands fast forever.

PSALM 125:1 AMP

One of the best ways to counteract stress is to pray for others.

TEMPTED

My Daughter,

When temptation knocks at your door, don't answer. It may offer a shortcut to your dreams, but there is a high price to pay. I am your strength when you are weak. Look to Me as your tower of strength to resist temptation, and take My hand and follow Me away from it. I will restore your faith and give you courage to overcome temptation so that your heart may continually please Me.

~God

No temptation has overtaken you that is not
common to man. God is faithful, and he will not
let you be tempted beyond your strength, but
with the temptation will also provide the way
of escape, that you may be able to endure it.
1 CORINTHIANS 10:13 RSV

Since he himself has now been through
suffering and temptation, he knows what
it is like when we suffer and are tempted,
and he is wonderfully able to help us.
HEBREWS 2:18 TLB

We do not have a High Priest who cannot sympathize
with our weaknesses, but was in all points tempted
as we are, yet without sin. Let us therefore come
boldly to the throne of grace, that we may obtain
mercy and find grace to help in time of need.
HEBREWS 4:15–16 NKJV

Blessed (happy, to be envied) is the man who is
patient under trial and stands up under temptation,
for when he has stood the test and been approved,
he will receive [the victor's] crown of life which
God has promised to those who love Him.
JAMES 1:12 AMP

Put on the whole armor of God, that you may be
able to stand against the wiles of the devil.
EPHESIANS 6:11 NKJV

People who love the Lord hate evil and
frees them from the power of the wicked.
PSALM 97:10 NCV

*Our response to temptation is an accurate
barometer of our love for God.*

WORRIED

My Daughter,

I know you are busy with your life and all the things so many depend on you to do. However, don't become distracted with so much serving that you forget to spend time with Me. Of all the things you consider as needs in your life that worry you, only one thing is most important—your time with Me. When you make time for Me, I will make time for all the really important things. I will show you what is necessary and what to leave behind in your day. Walk through your day with Me—and don't worry so much!

~God

I was very worried, but you comforted
me and made me happy.

PSALM 94:19 NCV

[Cast] all your anxiety on Him,
because He cares for you.

1 PETER 5:7 NASB

The fear of the Lord leads to life:
Then one rests content, untouched by trouble.

PROVERBS 19:23 NIV

"But seek first His kingdom and His righteousness,
and all these things will be added to you.
So do not worry about tomorrow;
for tomorrow will care for itself."

MATTHEW 6:33–34 NASB

God is greater than our worried hearts and
knows more about us than we do ourselves.

1 JOHN 3:20 THE MESSAGE

Anxiety weighs down the human heart,
but a good word cheers it up.

PROVERBS 12:25 NRSV

*Worry gives a small thing
a big shadow.*

GOD'S
PROMISES
CONCERNING . . .

FAITHFULNESS

My Daughter,

I assure you that I will be faithful to be
there for you. I am with you in times of
trouble and in times of peace. I will go
with you, and shelter you from the
storm and strengthen you with My
right hand. Don't be afraid of what lies
ahead, for My faithful presence will be
there with you. I am able to protect you
and keep you. When you ask, I will
answer. When you speak, I will listen.
I am faithful throughout eternity to be
your companion.

~God

The Lord passed in front of Moses and said,
"I am the Lord. The Lord is a God who shows mercy,
who is kind, who doesn't become angry quickly,
who has great love and faithfulness."

EXODUS 34:6 NCV

All the paths of the LORD are steadfast love
and faithfulness, for those who keep
his covenant and his testimonies.

PSALM 25:10 RSV

Your unfailing love will last forever.
Your faithfulness is as enduring as the heavens.

PSALM 89:2 NLT

O LORD, thou art my God; I will exalt thee,
I will praise thy name; for thou hast
done wonderful things; thy counsels
of old are faithfulness and truth.

ISAIAH 25:1 KJV

Hear my prayer, O Lord, give ear to
my supplications! In Your faithfulness
answer me, and in Your righteousness.

PSALM 143:1 AMP

He will cover you with His pinions,
and under His wings you may seek refuge;
His faithfulness is a shield and bulwark.

PSALM 91:4 NASB

I *do not pray for success,
I ask for faithfulness.*

FRIENDSHIP

My Daughter,

I want you to have friends who will love and honor you just as you love and honor them. I will bring those quality friendships into your life. Love them as you love Me. Give yourself to them sacrificially, not only looking after your own interest but also looking after their best interests. I will knit your hearts together as you include Me in your relationships. Appreciate those friendships I bring your way for they are for your blessing and happiness.

~God

Share each other's troubles and problems,
and in this way obey the law of Christ.

GALATIANS 6:2 NLT

A man who has friends must himself be friendly,
But there is a friend who
sticks closer than a brother.

PROVERBS 18:24 NKJV

Whoever loves his brother [believer] abides (lives)
in the Light, and in It or in him there is no
occasion for stumbling or cause for error or sin.

1 JOHN 2:10 AMP

Spend time with the wise and
you will become wise.

PROVERBS 13:20 NCV

A friend is always loyal, and a brother
is born to help in time of need.

PROVERBS 17:17 NLT

I call you not servants; for the servant knoweth
not what his lord doeth: but I have called you
friends; for all things that I have heard of my
Father I have made known unto you.

JOHN 15:15 KJV

Friendship is a serious affection;
the most sublime of all affections,
because it is founded on principle,
and cemented by time.

GENTLENESS

My Daughter,

My gentleness makes you great. So, let My meekness create in you a spirit of gentleness. For what this world needs is the gentle touch of My love through your life. Combine gentle words with kind acts that reveal My goodness for those around you. Treat them with the gentleness with which I treat you.

~God

The meek will inherit the land
and enjoy great peace.
PSALM 37:11 NIV

You have given me the shield of your salvation;
your gentleness has made me great.
2 SAMUEL 22:36 TLB

Pursue righteousness, godliness, faith, love,
endurance and gentleness. Fight the good fight of
the faith. Take hold of the eternal life to which
you were called when you made your good
confession in the presence of many witnesses.
1 TIMOTHY 6:11-12 NIV

When the Holy Spirit controls our lives he will
produce this kind of fruit in us: love, joy, peace,
patience, kindness, goodness, faithfulness,
gentleness and self-control.
GALATIANS 5:22-23 TLB

Which do you want: that I come to you with
punishment or with love and gentleness?
1 CORINTHIANS 4:21 NCV

Let everyone see that you are gentle
and kind. The Lord is coming soon.
PHILIPPIANS 4:5 NCV

*Children learn to care
by experiencing good care.
They come to know the blessings of
gentleness . . . through the way in
which they themselves are treated.*

HEAVEN

My Daughter,

When you have completed all that I
have for you to do on earth, then you
will join Me in Heaven. I have a place
prepared for you when it is time for you
to come to Me, and it is filled with
many treasures. It is My home and I
want to share it with you for eternity.
There are many things close to My
heart that I will share with you—
things that cannot be revealed at this
time, but are reserved for you in
Heaven. I love you and I love spending
time with you, on earth now, and in
the days to come, in Heaven.

~God

We know that when this earthly tent we live in is
taken down—when we die and leave these bodies—
we will have a home in heaven, an eternal body made
for us by God himself and not by human hands.

2 CORINTHIANS 5:1 NLT

"There are many rooms in my Father's house;
I would not tell you this if it were not true.
I am going there to prepare a place for you."

JOHN 14:2 NCV

"I tell you this: Whatever you prohibit on earth
is prohibited in heaven, and whatever you
allow on earth is allowed in heaven."

MATTHEW 18:18 NLT

This world is not our home; we are looking forward
to our city in heaven, which is yet to come.

HEBREWS 13:14 NLT

"Do not store up for yourselves treasures on earth,
where moth and rust destroy, and where thieves break
in and steal. But store up for yourselves treasures in
heaven, where neither moth nor rust destroys, and
where thieves do not break in or steal; for where
your treasure is, there your heart will be also."

MATTHEW 6:19–21 NASB

Blessed be the God and Father of our Lord Jesus Christ,
who according to His abundant mercy has begotten
us again to a living hope through the resurrection
of Jesus Christ from the dead, to an inheritance
incorruptible and undefiled and that does not
fade away, reserved in heaven for you, who
are kept by the power of God through faith for salvation
ready to be revealed in the last time.

1 PETER 1:3–5 NKJV

@

*Heaven is large, and affords space for
all modes of love and fortitude.*

149

HIS LOVE

My Daughter,

You are a treasure to Me of the greatest value. My love for you far exceeds anything of measure. It is more vast than the oceans, more immeasurable than the sands near the sea. I love you with an everlasting love. I want to hear about your dreams and share all of your life with you. I knew you before you were born, and I have great plans for you. I will never leave you and will love you throughout eternity.

~God

"God so loved the world that he gave his only Son,
so that everyone who believes in him may
not perish but may have eternal life."
JOHN 3:16 NRSV

"I have loved you even as the Father has loved me.
Remain in my love. When you obey me,
you remain in my love, just as I obey
my Father and remain in his love."
JOHN 15:9-10 NLT

Let us love one another, for love is from God;
and everyone who loves is born of God and
knows God. The one who does not love
does not know God, for God is love.
1 JOHN 4:7-8 NASB

We need have no fear of someone who loves us
perfectly; his perfect love for us eliminates all dread
of what he might do to us. If we are afraid, it is for
fear of what he might do to us, and shows that we
are not fully convinced that he really loves us.
1 JOHN 4:18 TLB

"I have loved you, my people, with an everlasting
love. With unfailing love I have drawn you to myself."
JEREMIAH 31:3 NLT

How priceless is your unfailing love! Both high and low
among men find refuge in the shadow of your wings.
PSALM 36:7 NIV

❧

*Love is life. All, everything that I understand, I
understand only because I love. Everything is,
everything exists, only because I love. Everything
is united by it alone. Love is God, and to
die means that I, a particle of love, shall return
to the general and eternal source.*

151

HIS PRESENCE

My Daughter,

I am with you always. My presence will go with you every day. Come and sit with Me and experience sweet fellowship—for in My presence is fullness of joy. I find it so refreshing when you rest in My arms after a weary day. In My presence you will find the peace you're looking for. I have everything you need, so come to Me and allow Me to fill you with all that I am.

~God

Your ears will hear a word behind you,
"This is the way, walk in it," whenever
you turn to the right or to the left.

ISAIAH 30:21 NASB

"Remember, your Father knows exactly
what you need even before you ask him!"

MATTHEW 6:8 TLB

"Where two or three have gathered together
in My name, I am there in their midst."

MATTHEW 18:20 NASB

My presence shall go *with thee*,
and I will give thee rest.

EXODUS 33:14 ASV

"Be sure of this—that I am with you always,
even to the end of the world."

MATTHEW 28:20 TLB

I cried out to the LORD in my suffering, and he
heard me. He set me free from all my fears.
For the angel of the LORD guards all who fear him,
and he rescues them.

PSALM 34:6-7 NLT

*The glory of God is a living man; and the life
of man consists in beholding God.*

HIS WORD

My Daughter,

Allow My Word to be a lamp unto your feet and a light unto your path. With it you will never be in darkness, for it will light your way. My Word will never pass away; you can count on the promises I make for eternity. It will not fail you but it will accomplish all that it is sent forth to do. My Word is established forever. Put it into your heart so that you can become strong and secure in Me. Then do what it says, so that your life will reflect My power.

~God

"It is written in the Scriptures, 'A person
does not live by eating only bread,
but by everything God says.'"

MATTHEW 4:4 NCV

Blessed are they that hear the
word of God, and keep it.

LUKE 11:28 ASV

"Heaven and earth shall disappear,
but my words stand sure forever."

MARK 13:31 TLB

Thy word is a lamp unto my feet,
and light unto my path.

PSALM 119:105 ASV

Do what God's teaching says; when you only listen
and do nothing, you are fooling yourselves.

JAMES 1:22 NCV

The word of God is living and powerful, and
sharper than any two-edged sword, piercing
even to the division of soul and spirit, and
of joints and marrow, and is a discerner of
the thoughts and intents of the heart.

HEBREWS 4:12 NKJV

*A Bible that's falling apart probably belongs
to someone who isn't.*

HONOR

My Daughter,

When you honor Me, I will honor you.
When you seek My face and do My Word,
you bring honor to Me. And those who
follow Me and serve Me will receive My
honor. So, call upon Me. I will answer
you; I will be with you in trouble, I will
deliver you and honor you.

~God

A person who refuses correction will end up
poor and disgraced, but the one who
accepts correction will be honored.

PROVERBS 13:18 NCV

Keep traveling steadily along [the Lord's]
pathway and in due season he will
honor you with every blessing.

PSALM 37:34 TLB

They that be wise shall shine as the brightness
of the firmament; and they that turn many to
righteousness as the stars for ever and ever.

DANIEL 12:3 KJV

You have made him a little lower than the angels,
and You have crowned him with glory and honor.

PSALM 8:5 NKJV

Honor the Lord by giving him the first part of
all your income, and he will fill your barns
with wheat and barley and overflow your
wine vats with the finest wines.

PROVERBS 3:9-10 TLB

[Jesus said,] "Whoever serves me must follow me;
and where I am, my servant also will be.
My Father will honor the one who serves me."

JOHN 12:26 NIV

*Our own heart and not other men's
opinions, form true honor.*

INTEGRITY

My Daughter,

The world tells you that prosperity comes to those who aggressively seek advancement, no matter what the cost. I say to you, walk before Me with integrity of heart, doing according to all that I have asked of you. In keeping My commandments, I will establish you. Live a life of integrity, and you will be secure in all you do. Do not seek public acclaim, or wealth, but rather serve Me and those I call you to with integrity of heart. For there you will find true riches.

~God

He who walks in integrity walks securely.

PROVERBS 10:9 RSV

As for you, if you will walk before me, as David your father walked, with integrity of heart and uprightness, doing according to all that I have commanded you, and keeping my statutes and my ordinances, then I will establish your royal throne over Israel for ever, as I promised.

1 KINGS 9:4-5 RSV

By standing firm you will gain life.

LUKE 21:19 NIV

The integrity of the upright will guide them.

PROVERBS 11:3 NASB

May integrity and honesty protect me,
for I put my hope in you.

PSALM 25:21 NLT

In my integrity you uphold me and set me in your presence forever.

PSALM 41:12 NIV

*A good name keeps its brightness
even in dark days.*

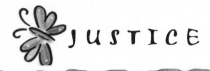 # JUSTICE

My Child,

Walk justly, but do not judge. It is not for you to judge or take revenge on those who mistreat you. Rather, I call you to entrust yourself to Me, for I am the One who judges justly. And I will take care of you. When you do right when you are unjustly treated, you honor Me by not retaliating. You act like My Son, for He did not open His mouth in retaliation, but entrusted himself to Me. In the end, you will see justice served. Fear not. I will help you.

~God

"He does not crush the weak, or quench the smallest hope; He will end all conflict with his final victory, and his name shall be the hope of all the world."
MATTHEW 12:20 TLB

God presented him as a sacrifice of atonement, through faith in his blood. He did this to demonstrate his justice, because in his forbearance he had left the sins committed beforehand unpunished— he did it to demonstrate his justice at the present time, so as to be just and the one who justifies those who have faith in Jesus.
ROMANS 3:25-26 NIV

"Justice, and only justice, you shall pursue, that you may live and possess the land which the LORD your God is giving you."
DEUTERONOMY 16:20 NASB

Then my enemies will retreat in the day when I call. This I know, that God is for me.
PSALM 56:9 NRSV

You prepare a feast for me in the presence of my enemies.
PSALM 23:5 NLT

"Behold, all those who were incensed against you shall be ashamed and disgraced; they shall be as nothing, and those who strive with you shall perish. You shall seek them and not find them—those who contended with you. Those who war against you shall be as nothing, as a nonexistent thing. For I, the Lord your God, will hold your right hand, saying to you, 'Fear not, I will help you.'"
ISAIAH 41:11-13 NKJV

*J*ustice consists in doing no injury to men; decency in giving them no offence.

KINDNESS

My Daughter,

My heart is forever toward you. With an everlasting kindness will I have mercy on you, and I will show you My marvelous love. I stand ready to pardon all who ask for forgiveness. I will never forsake those who come to Me. So, seek me with all your heart and let Me fill you with My Spirit. Let My goodness and kindness fill your life with salvation, healing and love.

~God

Give thanks to the LORD, for He is good;
for His lovingkindness is everlasting.
PSALM 118:1 NASB

His merciful kindness is great toward us.
PSALM 117:2 KJV

When the kindness and the love of God our
Savior toward man appeared, not by works of
righteousness which we have done, but according
to His mercy He saved us, through the washing of
regeneration and renewing of the Holy Spirit.
TITUS 3:4-5 NKJV

In a little burst of wrath I hid My face from you
for a moment, but with age-enduring love and
kindness I will have compassion and mercy
on you, says the Lord, your Redeemer.
ISAIAH 54:8 AMP

They refused to obey, and were not mindful of the
wonders that you performed among them; but they
stiffened their necks and determined to return to their
slavery in Egypt. But you are a God ready to forgive,
gracious and merciful, slow to anger and abounding
in steadfast love, and you did not forsake them.
NEHEMIAH 9:17 NRSV

Praise the Lord. His love to me was wonderful
when my city was attacked. In my distress,
I said, "God cannot see me!" But you heard
my prayer when I cried out to you for help.
PSALM 31:21-22 NCV

*The best portions of a good man's life [are]
his little nameless, unremembered acts of
kindness and love.*

163

LOVE

My Daughter,

I have loved you with an everlasting love. I love you so much that I call you My very own child. I gave My only begotten Son for you that you may have eternal life and fellowship with Me forever. Love never stops, but selflessly put others first. Love doesn't force itself on others and say, "Look at me!" Love is even tempered. It doesn't keep score. Love always trusts Me. Love never looks back but steps up and presses on to the end. I am love. And when you choose to dwell in Me, I shall love others through you.

~God

Most important of all, continue to show deep love for each other, for love makes up for many of your faults.
1 PETER 4:8 TLB

Most important, love each other. Love is what holds you all together in perfect unity.
COLOSSIANS 3:14 NCV

Many sorrows come to the wicked, but abiding love surrounds those who trust in the Lord.
PSALM 32:10 TLB

There are three things that will endure—faith, hope, and love—and the greatest of these is love.
1 CORINTHIANS 13:13 NLT

If you love someone you will be loyal to him no matter what the cost. You will always believe in him, always expect the best of him, and always stand your ground in defending him.
1 CORINTHIANS 13:7 TLB

May the Lord make your love increase and overflow for each other and for everyone else, just as ours does for you.
1 THESSALONIANS 3:12 NIV

Love feels no burden, thinks nothing of trouble, attempts what is above its strength, pleads no excuse of impossibility; for it thinks all things lawful for itself, and all things possible. It is therefore able to undertake all things, and warrants them to take effect, where he who does not love, would faint and lie down.

PRAYER

My Daughter,

Communication with you is important to My relationship with you. I love it when you talk to Me about your life, your hopes and your dreams. Pray without ceasing, for I am always here to listen and respond to your prayers. I enjoy the time you spend with Me in prayer—earnest prayer for a need you have, prayers of thanksgiving and praise, and times when you simply want to talk to Me. You can pray at any time. You don't need an invitation or a formal occasion to pray. Just come to Me; I am always here waiting for you.

~God

"When you pray, go away by yourself, all alone,
and shut the door behind you and pray
to your Father secretly, and your Father,
who knows your secrets, will reward you."

MATTHEW 6:6 TLB

"Even before they finish praying to me,
I will answer their prayers."

ISAIAH 65:24 TEV

The earnest prayer of a righteous person
has great power and wonderful results.

JAMES 5:16 NLT

My voice shalt thou hear in the morning,
O LORD; in the morning will I direct my
prayer unto thee, and will look up.

PSALM 5:3 KJV

While Jesus lived on earth, he prayed to God and
asked God for help. He prayed with loud cries and
tears to the One who could save him from death,
and his prayer was heard because he trusted God.

HEBREWS 5:7 NCV

"And all things you ask in prayer,
believing, you will receive."

MATTHEW 21:22 NASB

☙

*I need to stop talking about
prayer and pray.*

RECONCILIATION

My Daughter,

As I have forgiven you, now you must forgive others. I have reconciled you to myself through Jesus' death, burial, and resurrection. And through My great mercy and love you, too, can forgive others and reconcile with them. I have given you the ability to love them. I have poured out My own love in your heart so that you might love them with My love. You can do it. I will help you. Step out in faith and I will meet you.

~God

Not only this, but we also exult in God through
our Lord Jesus Christ, through whom we
have now received the reconciliation.

ROMANS 5:11 NASB

Be kind and compassionate to one another, forgiving
each other, just as in Christ God forgave you.

EPHESIANS 4:32 NIV

In Christ God was reconciling the world to himself,
not counting their trespasses against them, and
entrusting the message of reconciliation to us.

2 CORINTHIANS 5:19 NRSV

"Rebuke your brother if he sins, and
forgive him if he is sorry."

LUKE 17:3 TLB

It was the Father's good pleasure for all the
fullness to dwell in Him, and through Him to
reconcile all things to Himself, having made peace
through the blood of His cross; through Him, I say,
whether things on earth or things in heaven.

COLOSSIANS 1:19-20 NASB

He Himself is our peace, who has made both one,
and has broken down the middle wall of separation,
having abolished in His flesh the enmity, that is, the
law of commandments contained in ordinances, so
as to create in Himself one new man from the two,
thus making peace, and that He might reconcile
them both to God in one body through the cross,
thereby putting to death the enmity.

EPHESIANS 2:14-16 NKJV

*C*hrist comes to bind lives to God through reconciliation.
*He comes to bind human lives closely to one another in
fellowship. He comes to bind up the individual human life
that is lost and divided. Christian unity involves all these
three aspects of peace.*

169

RELATIONSHIPS

My Daughter,

I want your relationships with others to
reflect your relationship with Me. I am
loving, gentle, merciful, and kind; and
so should you be. When you forgive
others, encourage others, and appreciate
their individuality, your life is a
reflection to others of the way I have
treated you. When others look at you, I
want them to see Me through you. As
you grow, build lasting relationships by
following My example. I will help you
relate to others from a pure heart if you
will come to Me for help.

~God

"Again, truly I tell you, if two of you agree on earth about anything you ask, it will be done for you by my Father in heaven. For where two or three are gathered in my name, I am there among them."
MATTHEW 18:19-20 NRSV

Servants, do what you're told by your earthly masters. And don't just do the minimum that will get you by. Do your best. Work from the heart for your real Master, for God, confident that you'll get paid in full when you come into your inheritance. Keep in mind always that the ultimate Master you're serving is Christ.
COLOSSIANS 3:22-24 THE MESSAGE

Now you can have real love for everyone because your souls have been cleansed from selfishness and hatred when you trusted Christ to save you; so see to it that you really do love each other warmly, with all your hearts.
1 PETER 1:22 TLB

Share each other's troubles and problems, and in this way obey the law of Christ.
GALATIANS 6:2 NLT

Never abandon a friend—either yours or your father's. Then you won't need to go to a distant relative for help in your time of need.
PROVERBS 27:10 TLB

Two people can accomplish more than twice as much as one; they get a better return for their labor. If one person falls, the other can reach out and help. But people who are alone when they fall are in real trouble. And on a cold night, two under the same blanket can gain warmth from each other. But how can one be warm alone? A person standing alone can be attacked and defeated, but two can stand back-to-back and conquer. Three are even better, for a triple-braided cord is not easily broken.
ECCLESIASTES 4:9-12 NLT

If we would build on a sure foundation in friendship, we must love our friends for their sakes rather than our own.

TRUST

My Daughter,

Trust Me with your life and all that concerns you, for I love you completely and want to lead you down the path of life. I rescued you from darkness and brought you into the light. I will protect you and will not allow you to be disgraced for I am your strength and shield from danger. I am able to deliver you out of all your troubles. I sent My Son to give you life abundant and eternal. With Him I will freely give you all the good things that I have promised you in My Word. Will you trust Me?

~God

Trust in the L<small>ORD</small> with all your heart and
lean not on your own understanding;
in all your ways acknowledge him,
and he will make your paths straight

PROVERBS 3:5-6 NIV

Those who know your name trust in you,
for you, O L<small>ORD</small>, have never abandoned
anyone who searches for you.

PSALM 9:10 NLT

He who trusts in the L<small>ORD</small> will prosper.

PROVERBS 28:25 NIV

Blessed are all those who put their trust in Him.

PSALM 2:12 NKJV

In God I have put my trust, I shall not be afraid.

PSALM 56:11 NASB

It is better to trust the L<small>ORD</small> than to trust people.

PSALM 118:8 NCV

*I would rather walk with God in the dark
than go alone in the light.*

TRUTH

My Daughter,

Don't look for easy answer from those
who tell you what you want to hear.
Follow My path, for I have called you
to live in truth. Love the truth, and
purify yourself by obeying it. Seek the
truth, and follow it passionately, for
the way of truth leads to life
everlasting. For My truth sets you free.

~God

Guide me in your truth and teach me, for you are
God my Savior, and my hope is in you all day long.

PSALM 25:5 NIV

Now that you have purified yourselves by
obeying the truth so that you have sincere love
for your brothers, love one another deeply,
from the heart. For you have been born again,
not of perishable seed, but of imperishable,
through the living and enduring word of God.

1 PETER 1:22–23 NIV

Your righteousness is everlasting and your law is true.

PSALM 119:142 NIV

"When he, the Spirit of truth, comes,
he will guide you into all truth."

JOHN 16:13 NIV

Meanwhile, we've got our hands full continually
thanking God for you, our good friends—so loved by
God! God picked you out as his from the very start.
Think of it: included in God's original plan of
salvation by the bond of faith in the living truth.

2 THESSALONIANS 2:13 THE MESSAGE

Behold, You desire truth in the inner being; make
me therefore to know wisdom in my inmost heart.

PSALM 51:6 AMP

*Truth is always in harmony with herself, and
is not concerned chiefly to reveal the justice
that may consist with wrong-doing.*

WORK

My Daughter,

Work hard and cheerfully in all that you do as though you were working for Me and not for those in leadership over you. Remember that I am the One who will give you your reward—not them. So, work cheerfully and diligently for Me, and I will bless the work of your hands and reward you with the rich inheritance that I have reserved and prepared for you.

~God

God has promised us a Sabbath when we
will rest, even though it has not yet come.
On that day God's people will rest from
their work, just as God rested from his work.
HEBREWS 4:9-10 CEV

Servants, respectfully obey your earthly masters but
always with an eye to obeying the real master, Christ.
Don't just do what you have to do to get by, but work
heartily, as Christ's servants doing what God wants
you to do. And work with a smile on your face,
always keeping in mind that no matter who happens
to be giving the orders, you're really serving God.
EPHESIANS 6:5-7 THE MESSAGE

Work hard and cheerfully at all you do, just as though
you were working for the Lord and not merely for your
masters, remembering that it is the Lord Christ who is
going to pay you, giving you your full portion of all
he owns. He is the one you are really working for.
COLOSSIANS 3:23-24 TLB

The generous prosper and are satisfied; those who
refresh others will themselves be refreshed.
PROVERBS 11:25 NLT

Whatever work you do, do your best.
ECCLESIASTES 9:10 NCV

The master said, "Well done, my good and faithful
servant. You have been faithful in handling this
small amount, so now I will give you many more
responsibilities. Let's celebrate together!"
MATTHEW 25:23 NLT

A task with vision is victory.

READ THROUGH
THE BIBLE IN
ONE YEAR

JANUARY

1. Genesis 1-2; Psalm 1; Matthew 1-2
2. Genesis 3-4; Psalm 2; Matthew 3-4
3. Genesis 5-7; Psalm 3; Matthew 5
4. Genesis 8-9; Psalm 4; Matthew 6-7
5. Genesis 10-11; Psalm 5; Matthew 8-9
6. Genesis 12-13; Psalm 6; Matthew 10-11
7. Genesis 14-15; Psalm 7; Matthew 12
8. Genesis 16-17; Psalm 8; Matthew 13
9. Genesis 18-19; Psalm 9; Matthew 14-15
10. Genesis 20-21; Psalm 10; Matthew 16-17
11. Genesis 22-23; Psalm 11; Matthew 18
12. Genesis 24; Psalm 12; Matthew 19-20
13. Genesis 25-26; Psalm 13; Matthew 21
14. Genesis 27-28; Psalm 14; Matthew 22
15. Genesis 29-30; Psalm 15; Matthew 23
16. Genesis 31-32; Psalm 16; Matthew 24
17. Genesis 33-34; Psalm 17; Matthew 25
18. Genesis 35-36; Psalm 18; Matthew 26
19. Genesis 37-38; Psalm 19; Matthew 27
20. Genesis 39-40; Psalm 20; Matthew 28
21. Genesis 41-42; Psalm 21; Mark 1
22. Genesis 43-44; Psalm 22; Mark 2
23. Genesis 45-46; Psalm 23; Mark 3
24. Genesis 47-48; Psalm 24; Mark 4
25. Genesis 49-50; Psalm 25; Mark 5
26. Exodus 1-2; Psalm 26; Mark 6
27. Exodus 3-4; Psalm 27; Mark 7
28. Exodus 5-6; Psalm 28; Mark 8
29. Exodus 7-8; Psalm 29; Mark 9
30. Exodus 9-10; Psalm 30; Mark 10
31. Exodus 11-12; Psalm 31; Mark 11

FEBRUARY

1. Exodus 13-14; Psalm 32; Mark 12
2. Exodus 15-16; Psalm 33; Mark 13
3. Exodus 17-18; Psalm 34; Mark 14
4. Exodus 19-20; Psalm 35; Mark 15
5. Exodus 21-22; Psalm 36; Mark 16
6. Exodus 23-24; Psalm 37; Luke 1
7. Exodus 25-26; Psalm 38; Luke 2
8. Exodus 27-28; Psalm 39; Luke 3
9. Exodus 29-30; Psalm 40; Luke 4
10. Exodus 31-32; Psalm 41; Luke 5
11. Exodus 33-34; Psalm 42; Luke 6
12. Exodus 35-36; Psalm 43; Luke 7
13. Exodus 37-38; Psalm 44; Luke 8
14. Exodus 39-40; Psalm 45; Luke 9
15. Leviticus 1-2; Psalm 46; Luke 10
16. Leviticus 3-4; Psalm 47; Luke 11
17. Leviticus 5-6; Psalm 48; Luke 12
18. Leviticus 7-8; Psalm 49; Luke 13
19. Leviticus 9-10; Psalm 50; Luke 14
20. Leviticus 11-12; Psalm 51; Luke 15
21. Leviticus 13; Psalm 52; Luke 16
22. Leviticus 14; Psalm 53; Luke 17
23. Leviticus 15-16; Psalm 54; Luke 18
24. Leviticus 17-18; Psalm 55; Luke 19
25. Leviticus 19-20; Psalm 56; Luke 20
26. Leviticus 21-22; Psalm 57; Luke 21
27. Leviticus 23-24; Psalm 58; Luke 22
28. Leviticus 25; Psalm 59; Luke 23

MARCH

1. Leviticus 26-27; Psalm 60; Luke 24
2. Numbers 1-2; Psalm 61; John 1
3. Numbers 3-4; Psalm 62; John 2-3
4. Numbers 5-6; Psalm 63; John 4
5. Numbers 7; Psalm 64; John 5
6. Numbers 8-9; Psalm 65; John 6
7. Numbers 10-11; Psalm 66; John 7
8. Numbers 12-13; Psalm 67; John 8
9. Numbers 14-15; Psalm 68; John 9
10. Numbers 16; Psalm 69; John 10
11. Numbers 17-18; Psalm 70; John 11
12. Numbers 19-20; Psalm 71; John 12
13. Numbers 21-22; Psalm 72; John 13
14. Numbers 23-24; Psalm 73; John 14-15
15. Numbers 25-26; Psalm 74; John 16
16. Numbers 27-28; Psalm 75; John 17
17. Numbers 29-30; Psalm 76; John 18
18. Numbers 31-32; Psalm 77; John 19
19. Numbers 33-34; Psalm 78; John 20
20. Numbers 35-36; Psalm 79; John 21
21. Deuteronomy 1-2; Psalm 80; Acts 1
22. Deuteronomy 3-4; Psalm 81; Acts 2
23. Deuteronomy 5-6; Psalm 82; Acts 3-4
24. Deuteronomy 7-8; Psalm 83; Acts 5-6
25. Deuteronomy 9-10; Psalm 84; Acts 7
26. Deuteronomy 11-12; Psalm 85; Acts 8
27. Deuteronomy 13-14; Psalm 86; Acts 9
28. Deuteronomy 15-16; Psalm 87; Acts 10
29. Deuteronomy 17-18; Psalm 88; Acts 11-12
30. Deuteronomy 19-20; Psalm 89; Acts 13
31. Deuteronomy 21-22; Psalm 90; Acts 14

APRIL

1. Deuteronomy 23-24; Psalm 91; Acts 15
2. Deuteronomy 25-27; Psalm 92; Acts 16
3. Deuteronomy 28-29; Psalm 93; Acts 17
4. Deuteronomy 30-31; Psalm 94; Acts 18
5. Deuteronomy 32; Psalm 95; Acts 19
6. Deuteronomy 33-34; Psalm 96; Acts 20
7. Joshua 1-2; Psalm 97; Acts 21
8. Joshua 3-4; Psalm 98; Acts 22
9. Joshua 5-6; Psalm 99; Acts 23
10. Joshua 7-8; Psalm 100; Acts 24-25
11. Joshua 9-10; Psalm 101; Acts 26
12. Joshua 11-12; Psalm 102; Acts 27
13. Joshua 13-14; Psalm 103; Acts 28
14. Joshua 15-16; Psalm 104; Romans 1-2
15. Joshua 17-18; Psalm 105; Romans 3-4
16. Joshua 19-20; Psalm 106; Romans 5-6
17. Joshua 21-22; Psalm 107; Romans 7-8
18. Joshua 23-24; Psalm 108; Romans 9-10
19. Judges 1-2; Psalm 109; Romans 11-12
20. Judges 3-4; Psalm 110; Romans 13-14
21. Judges 5-6; Psalm 111; Romans 15-16
22. Judges 7-8; Psalm 112; 1 Corinthians 1-2
23. Judges 9; Psalm 113; 1 Corinthians 3-4
24. Judges 10-11; Psalm 114; 1 Corinthians 5-6
25. Judges 12-13; Psalm 115; 1 Corinthians 7
26. Judges 14-15; Psalm 116; 1 Corinthians 8-9
27. Judges 16-17; Psalm 117; 1 Corinthians 10
28. Judges 18-19; Psalm 118; 1 Corinthians 11
29. Judges 20-21; Psalm 119:1-88; 1 Corinthians 12
30. Ruth 1-4; Psalm 119:89-176; 1 Corinthians 13

MAY

1. 1 Samuel 1-2; Psalm 120; 1 Corinthians 14
2. 1 Samuel 3-4; Psalm 121; 1 Corinthians 15
3. 1 Samuel 5-6; Psalm 122; 1 Corinthians 16
4. 1 Samuel 7-8; Psalm 123; 2 Corinthians 1
5. 1 Samuel 9-10; Psalm 124; 2 Corinthians 2-3
6. 1 Samuel 11-12; Psalm 125; 2 Corinthians 4-5
7. 1 Samuel 13-14; Psalm 126; 2 Corinthians 6-7
8. 1 Samuel 15-16; Psalm 127; 2 Corinthians 8
9. 1 Samuel 17; Psalm 128; 2 Corinthians 9-10
10. 1 Samuel 18-19; Psalm 129; 2 Corinthians 11
11. 1 Samuel 20-21; Psalm 130; 2 Corinthians 12
12. 1 Samuel 22-23; Psalm 131; 2 Corinthians 13
13. 1 Samuel 24-25; Psalm 132; Galatians 1-2
14. 1 Samuel 26-27; Psalm 133; Galatians 3-4
15. 1 Samuel 28-29; Psalm 134; Galatians 5-6
16. 1 Samuel 30-31; Psalm 135; Ephesians 1-2
17. 2 Samuel 1-2; Psalm 136; Ephesians 3-4
18. 2 Samuel 3-4; Psalm 137; Ephesians 5-6
19. 2 Samuel 5-6; Psalm 138; Philippians 1-2
20. 2 Samuel 7-8; Psalm 139; Philippians 3-4
21. 2 Samuel 9-10; Psalm 140; Colossians 1-2
22. 2 Samuel 11-12; Psalm 141; Colossians 3-4
23. 2 Samuel 13-14; Psalm 142; 1 Thessalonians 1-2
24. 2 Samuel 15-16; Psalm 143; 1 Thessalonians 3-4
25. 2 Samuel 17-18; Psalm 144; 1 Thessalonians 5
26. 2 Samuel 19; Psalm 145; 2 Thessalonians 1-3
27. 2 Samuel 20-21; Psalm 146; 1 Timothy 1-2
28. 2 Samuel 22; Psalm 147; 1 Timothy 3-4
29. 2 Samuel 23-24; Psalm 148; 1 Timothy 5-6
30. 1 Kings 1; Psalm 149; 2 Timothy 1-2
31. 1 Kings 2-3; Psalm 150; 2 Timothy 3-4

JUNE

1. 1 Kings 4-5; Proverbs 1; Titus 1-3
2. 1 Kings 6-7; Proverbs 2; Philemon
3. 1 Kings 8; Proverbs 3; Hebrews 1-2
4. 1 Kings 9-10; Proverbs 4; Hebrews 3-4
5. 1 Kings 11-12; Proverbs 5; Hebrews 5-6
6. 1 Kings 13-14; Proverbs 6; Hebrews 7-8
7. 1 Kings 15-16; Proverbs 7; Hebrews 9-10
8. 1 Kings 17-18; Proverbs 8; Hebrews 11
9. 1 Kings 19-20; Proverbs 9; Hebrews 12
10. 1 Kings 21-22; Proverbs 10; Hebrews 13
11. 2 Kings 1-2; Proverbs 11; James 1
12. 2 Kings 3-4; Proverbs 12; James 2-3
13. 2 Kings 5-6; Proverbs 13; James 4-5
14. 2 Kings 7-8; Proverbs 14; 1 Peter 1
15. 2 Kings 9-10; Proverbs 15; 1 Peter 2-3
16. 2 Kings 11-12; Proverbs 16; 1 Peter 4-5
17. 2 Kings 13-14; Proverbs 17; 2 Peter 1-3
18. 2 Kings 15-16; Proverbs 18; 1 John 1-2
19. 2 Kings 17; Proverbs 19; 1 John 3-4
20. 2 Kings 18-19; Proverbs 20; 1 John 5
21. 2 Kings 20-21; Proverbs 21; 2 John
22. 2 Kings 22-23; Proverbs 22; 3 John
23. 2 Kings 24-25; Proverbs 23; Jude
24. 1 Chronicles 1; Proverbs 24; Revelation 1-2
25. 1 Chronicles 2-3; Proverbs 25; Revelation 3-5
26. 1 Chronicles 4-5; Proverbs 26; Revelation 6-7
27. 1 Chronicles 6-7; Proverbs 27; Revelation 8-10
28. 1 Chronicles 8-9; Proverbs 28; Revelation 11-12
29. 1 Chronicles 10-11; Proverbs 29; Revelation 13-14
30. 1 Chronicles 12-13; Proverbs 30, Revelation 15-17

JULY

1. 1 Chronicles 14-15; Proverbs 31; Revelation 18-19
2. 1 Chronicles 16-17; Psalm 1; Revelation 20-22
3. 1 Chronicles 18-19; Psalm 2; Matthew 1-2
4. 1 Chronicles 20-21; Psalm 3; Matthew 3-4
5. 1 Chronicles 22-23; Psalm 4; Matthew 5
6. 1 Chronicles 24-25; Psalm 5; Matthew 6-7
7. 1 Chronicles 26-27; Psalm 6; Matthew 8-9
8. 1 Chronicles 28-29; Psalm 7; Matthew 10-11
9. 2 Chronicles 1-2; Psalm 8; Matthew 12
10. 2 Chronicles 3-4; Psalm 9; Matthew 13
11. 2 Chronicles 5-6; Psalm 10; Matthew 14-15
12. 2 Chronicles 7-8; Psalm 11; Matthew 16-17
13. 2 Chronicles 9-10; Psalm 12; Matthew 18
14. 2 Chronicles 11-12; Psalm 13; Matthew 19-20
15. 2 Chronicles 13-14; Psalm 14; Matthew 21
16. 2 Chronicles 15-16; Psalm 15; Matthew 22
17. 2 Chronicles 17-18; Psalm 16; Matthew 23
18. 2 Chronicles 19-20; Psalm 17; Matthew 24
19. 2 Chronicles 21-22; Psalm 18; Matthew 25
20. 2 Chronicles 23-24; Psalm 19; Matthew 26
21. 2 Chronicles 25-26; Psalm 20; Matthew 27
22. 2 Chronicles 27-28; Psalm 21; Matthew 28
23. 2 Chronicles 29-30; Psalm 22; Mark 1
24. 2 Chronicles 31-32; Psalm 23; Mark 2
25. 2 Chronicles 33-34; Psalm 24; Mark 3
26. 2 Chronicles 35-36; Psalm 25; Mark 4
27. Ezra 1-2; Psalm 26; Mark 5
28. Ezra 3-4; Psalm 27; Mark 6
29. Ezra 5-6; Psalm 28; Mark 7
30. Ezra 7-8; Psalm 29; Mark 8
31. Ezra 9-10; Psalm 30; Mark 9

AUGUST

1. Nehemiah 1-2; Psalm 31; Mark 10
2. Nehemiah 3-4; Psalm 32; Mark 11
3. Nehemiah 5-6; Psalm 33; Mark 12
4. Nehemiah 7; Psalm 34; Mark 13
5. Nehemiah 8-9; Psalm 35; Mark 14
6. Nehemiah 10-11; Psalm 36; Mark 15
7. Nehemiah 12-13; Psalm 37; Mark 16
8. Esther 1-2; Psalm 38; Luke 1
9. Esther 3-4; Psalm 39; Luke 2
10. Esther 5-6; Psalm 40; Luke 3
11. Esther 7-8; Psalm 41; Luke 4
12. Esther 9-10; Psalm 42; Luke 5
13. Job 1-2; Psalm 43; Luke 6
14. Job 3-4; Psalm 44; Luke 7
15. Job 5-6; Psalm 45; Luke 8
16. Job 7-8; Psalm 46; Luke 9
17. Job 9-10; Psalm 47; Luke 10
18. Job 11-12; Psalm 48; Luke 11
19. Job 13-14; Psalm 49; Luke 12
20. Job 15-16; Psalm 50; Luke 13
21. Job 17-18; Psalm 51; Luke 14
22. Job 19-20; Psalm 52; Luke 15
23. Job 21-22; Psalm 53; Luke 16
24. Job 23-25; Psalm 54; Luke 17
25. Job 26-28; Psalm 55; Luke 18
26. Job 29-30; Psalm 56; Luke 19
27. Job 31-32; Psalm 57; Luke 20
28. Job 33-34; Psalm 58; Luke 21
29. Job 35-36; Psalm 59; Luke 22
30. Job 37-38; Psalm 60; Luke 23
31. Job 39-40; Psalm 61; Luke 24

SEPTEMBER

1. Job 41-42; Psalm 62; John 1
2. Ecclesiastes 1-2; Psalm 63; John 2-3
3. Ecclesiastes 3-4; Psalm 64; John 4
4. Ecclesiastes 5-6; Psalm 65; John 5
5. Ecclesiastes 7-8; Psalm 66; John 6
6. Ecclesiastes 9-10; Psalm 67; John 7
7. Ecclesiastes 11-12; Psalm 68; John 8
8. Song of Solomon 1-2; Psalm 69; John 9
9. Song of Solomon 3-4; Psalm 70; John 10
10. Song of Solomon 5-6; Psalm 71; John 11
11. Song of Solomon 7-8; Psalm 72; John 12
12. Isaiah 1-2; Psalm 73; John 13
13. Isaiah 3-5; Psalm 74; John 14-15
14. Isaiah 6-8; Psalm 75; John 16
15. Isaiah 9-10; Psalm 76; John 17
16. Isaiah 11-13; Psalm 77; John 18
17. Isaiah 14-15; Psalm 78; John 19
18. Isaiah 16-17; Psalm 79; John 20
19. Isaiah 18-19; Psalm 80; John 21
20. Isaiah 20-22; Psalm 81; Acts 1
21. Isaiah 23-24; Psalm 82; Acts 2
22. Isaiah 25-26; Psalm 83; Acts 3-4
23. Isaiah 27-28; Psalm 84; Acts 5-6
24. Isaiah 29-30; Psalm 85; Acts 7
25. Isaiah 31-32; Psalm 86; Acts 8
26. Isaiah 33-34; Psalm 87; Acts 9
27. Isaiah 35-36; Psalm 88; Acts 10
28. Isaiah 37-38; Psalm 89; Acts 11-12
29. Isaiah 39-40; Psalm 90; Acts 13
30. Isaiah 41-42; Psalm 91; Acts 14

OCTOBER

1. Isaiah 43-44; Psalm 92; Acts 15
2. Isaiah 45-46; Psalm 93; Acts 16
3. Isaiah 47-48; Psalm 94; Acts 17
4. Isaiah 49-50; Psalm 95; Acts 18
5. Isaiah 51-52; Psalm 96; Acts 19
6. Isaiah 53-54; Psalm 97; Acts 20
7. Isaiah 55-56; Psalm 98; Acts 21
8. Isaiah 57-58; Psalm 99; Acts 22
9. Isaiah 59-60; Psalm 100; Acts 23
10. Isaiah 61-62; Psalm 101; Acts 24-25
11. Isaiah 63-64; Psalm 102; Acts 26
12. Isaiah 65-66; Psalm 103; Acts 27
13. Jeremiah 1-2; Psalm 104; Acts 28
14. Jeremiah 3-4; Psalm 105; Romans 1-2
15. Jeremiah 5-6; Psalm 106; Romans 3-4
16. Jeremiah 7-8; Psalm 107; Romans 5-6
17. Jeremiah 9-10; Psalm 108; Romans 7-8
18. Jeremiah 11-12; Psalm 109; Romans 9-10
19. Jeremiah 13-14; Psalm 110; Romans 11-12
20. Jeremiah 15-16; Psalm 111; Romans 13-14
21. Jeremiah 17-18; Psalm 112; Romans 15-16
22. Jeremiah 19-20; Psalm 113; 1 Corinthians 1-2
23. Jeremiah 21-22; Psalm 114; 1 Corinthians 3-4
24. Jeremiah 23-24; Psalm 115; 1 Corinthians 5-6
25. Jeremiah 25-26; Psalm 116; 1 Corinthians 7
26. Jeremiah 27-28; Psalm 117; 1 Corinthians 8-9
27. Jeremiah 29-30; Psalm 118; 1 Corinthians 10
28. Jeremiah 31-32; Psalm 119: 1-64; 1 Corinthians 11
29. Jeremiah 33-34; Psalm 119:65-120; 1 Corinthians 12
30. Jeremiah 35-36; Psalm 119:121-176;1 Corinthians 13
31. Jeremiah 37-38; Psalm 120; 1 Corinthians 14

NOVEMBER

1. Jeremiah 39-40; Psalm 121; 1 Corinthians 15
2. Jeremiah 41-42; Psalm 122; 1 Corinthians 16
3. Jeremiah 43-44; Psalm 123; 2 Corinthians 1
4. Jeremiah 45-46; Psalm 124; 2 Corinthians 2-3
5. Jeremiah 47-48; Psalm 125; 2 Corinthians 4-5
6. Jeremiah 49-50; Psalm 126; 2 Corinthians 6-7
7. Jeremiah 51-52; Psalm 127; 2 Corinthians 8
8. Lamentations 1-2; Psalm 128; 2 Corinthians 9-10
9. Lamentations 3; Psalm 129; 2 Corinthians 11
10. Lamentations 4-5; Psalm 130; 2 Corinthians 12
11. Ezekiel 1-2; Psalm 131; 2 Corinthians 13
12. Ezekiel 3-4; Psalm 132; Galatians 1-2
13. Ezekiel 5-6; Psalm 133; Galatians 3-4
14. Ezekiel 7-8; Psalm 134; Galatians 5-6
15. Ezekiel 9-10; Psalm 135; Ephesians 1-2
16. Ezekiel 11-12; Psalm 136; Ephesians 3-4
17. Ezekiel 13-14; Psalm 137; Ephesians 5-6
18. Ezekiel 15-16; Psalm 138; Philippians 1-2
19. Ezekiel 17-18; Psalm 139; Philippians 3-4
20. Ezekiel 19-20; Psalm 140; Colossians 1-2
21. Ezekiel 21-22; Psalm 141; Colossians 3-4
22. Ezekiel 23-24; Psalm 142; 1 Thessalonians 1-2
23. Ezekiel 25-26; Psalm 143; 1 Thessalonians 3-4
24. Ezekiel 27-28; Psalm 144; 1 Thessalonians 5
25. Ezekiel 29-30; Psalm 145; 2 Thessalonians 1-3
26. Ezekiel 31-32; Psalm 146; 1 Timothy 1-2
27. Ezekiel 33-34; Psalm 147; 1 Timothy 3-4
28. Ezekiel 35-36; Psalm 148; 1 Timothy 5-6
29. Ezekiel 37-38; Psalm 149; 2 Timothy 1-2
30. Ezekiel 39-40; Psalm 150; 2 Timothy 3-4

DECEMBER

1. Ezekiel 41-42; Proverbs 1; Titus 1-3
2. Ezekiel 43-44; Proverbs 2; Philemon
3. Ezekiel 45-46; Proverbs 3; Hebrews 1-2
4. Ezekiel 47-48; Proverbs 4; Hebrews 3-4
5. Daniel 1-2; Proverbs 5; Hebrews 5-6
6. Daniel 3-4; Proverbs 6; Hebrews 7-8
7. Daniel 5-6; Proverbs 7; Hebrews 9-10
8. Daniel 7-8; Proverbs 8; Hebrews 11
9. Daniel 9-10; Proverbs 9; Hebrews 12
10. Daniel 11-12; Proverbs 10; Hebrews 13
11. Hosea 1-3; Proverbs 11; James 1-3
12. Hosea 4-6; Proverbs 12; James 4-5
13. Hosea 7-8; Proverbs 13; 1 Peter 1
14. Hosea 9-11; Proverbs 14; 1 Peter 2-3
15. Hosea 12-14; Proverbs 15; 1 Peter 4-5
16. Joel 1-3; Proverbs 16; 2 Peter 1-3
17. Amos 1-3; Proverbs 17; 1 John 1-2
18. Amos 4-6; Proverbs 18; 1 John 3-4
19. Amos 7-9; Proverbs 19; 1 John 5
20. Obadiah; Proverbs 20; 2 John
21. Jonah 1-4; Proverbs 21; 3 John
22. Micah 1-4; Proverbs 22; Jude
23. Micah 5-7; Proverbs 23; Revelation 1-2
24. Nahum 1-3; Proverbs 24; Revelation 3-5
25. Habakkuk 1-3; Proverbs 25; Revelation 6-7
26. Zephaniah 1-3; Proverbs 26; Revelation 8-10
27. Haggai 1-2; Proverbs 27; Revelation 11-12
28. Zechariah 1-4; Proverbs 28; Revelation 13-14
29. Zechariah 5-9; Proverbs 29; Revelation 15-17
30. Zechariah 10-14; Proverbs 30; Revelation 18-19
31. Malachi 1-4; Proverbs 31; Revelation 20-22